T0317595

Hedge Fund Compliance

Founded in 1807, John Wiley & Sons is the oldest independent publishing company in the United States. With offices in North America, Europe, Australia, and Asia, Wiley is globally committed to developing and marketing print and electronic products and services for our customers' professional and personal knowledge and understanding.

The Wiley Finance series contains books written specifically for finance and investment professionals as well as sophisticated individual investors and their financial advisors. Book topics range from portfolio management to e-commerce, risk management, financial engineering, valuation and financial instrument analysis, as well as much more.

For a list of available titles, visit our Web site at www.WileyFinance.com.

Hedge Fund Compliance

Risks, Regulation, and Management

JASON SCHARFMAN

WILEY

For general information on our other products and services or for technical support, please contact our Customer Care Department within the United States at (800) 762-2974, outside the United States at (317) 572-3993 or fax (317) 572-4002.

Wiley publishes in a variety of print and electronic formats and by print-on-demand. Some material included with standard print versions of this book may not be included in e-books or in print-on-demand. If this book refers to media such as a CD or DVD that is not included in the version you purchased, you may download this material at http://booksupport.wiley.com. For more information about Wiley products, visit www.wiley.com.

Library of Congress Cataloging-in-Publication Data is available

ISBN 978-1-119-24023-5 (Hardcover)
ISBN 978-1-119-24027-3 (ePDF)
ISBN 978-1-119-24026-6 (ePub)

Cover Design: Wiley
Cover Images: (top) © g0d4ather/Shutterstock; (bottom) © Rawpixel.com/Shutterstock

Printed in the United States of America

10 9 8 7 6 5 4 3 2 1

For R, Y, and Z

for R, J, and Z

Contents

Preface

Compliance is one of the fastest-growing areas in the hedge fund industry. Contributing to this change is a seemingly steady drumbeat of new global regulatory activity. In the United States and in Asia, for example, regulators have steadily enhanced their hedge fund compliance enforcement and surveillance activities. In Europe, broad shifts in the laws, such as the Alternative Investment Fund Managers Directive (AIFMD) and the Markets in Financial Instruments Directive (MiFID), have directly influenced the way hedge funds carry out their investment activities.

Today, hedge fund compliance has evolved into more than simply a regulatory exercise. Hedge fund compliance programs are now required to regularly engage compliance risks across a wide variety of operational and investment areas, ranging from cybersecurity and conflict of interest management to trade allocation and increased oversight of the use of investment research. To meet these challenges, hedge funds and their investors and service providers must continually reevaluate the role of the compliance function to ensure that they not only meet these new regulatory requirements but also keep pace with industry best practices. This book is written to assist these groups in embracing this challenge.

Readers of this book will come from different levels of sophistication, ranging from those in an academic setting and new to hedge fund industry to experienced hedge fund compliance professionals working in the compliance field. To assist in highlighting important compliance terminology as you read through each of the chapters, you will find key terms italicized and in boldface. Regardless of your previous compliance experience, this book can also serve as a reference source on specific compliance topics. To facilitate this, the chapters of this book have been organized by key compliance topic area for ease of navigation.

Specifically, this book is structured to provide an understanding of the core concepts of hedge fund compliance across three sections. The first section, Chapters 1 through 4, focuses on topics relating to the structure and duties of a hedge fund's internal compliance function. It begins by providing an introduction to the compliance function and the role of regulators. The Chief Compliance Officer (CCO) role, as well as the responsibilities of other shared and dedicated compliance personnel, are then discussed. This section concludes with an analysis of the function of internal compliance mechanisms, such as fund committees.

The second section of the book, Chapters 5 through 8, focuses on specific topics in compliance as well as the role of third parties in the process. This section begins by addressing the emerging role of technology in compliance management. The use of technology in performing a wide variety of compliance activities, including trade surveillance, archiving, and monitoring employee communications, is also covered. Next, the role of third parties that assist in compliance management, including compliance consultants, is discussed. Examples of key compliance documentation, including the Compliance Manual and Code of Ethics, are then presented. Finally, the process by which prospective and existing investors conduct due diligence on hedge fund compliance functions is addressed with a focus on the analysis of compliance policies regarding employee personal account dealing and material non-public information (MNPI).

The third and final section of the book, Chapters 9 through 12, applies critical compliance concepts directly to the real world. It begins by focusing on historical case studies and illustrative scenarios as well as common compliance pitfalls. Interviews with third-party compliance service providers are presented to demonstrate the practical opportunities and challenges facing hedge funds in working with third parties to implement and manage their compliance programs. Finally, the book concludes with a discussion of emerging topics and trends in the compliance space.

Compliance has evolved from a rote exercise of strictly following regulatory rules to one of the most prominent, dynamic, and multidisciplinary areas of hedge fund management. A strong compliance program can improve the overall operating efficiency and level of communication throughout a hedge fund. Similarly, hedge fund investors benefit from the additional oversight and transparency that comprehensive compliance programs can provide. Regardless of your role in the hedge fund industry, as compliance continues to evolve, developing a fundamental understanding of core compliance concepts is now an essential requirement for success.

Jason Scharfman
December 2016

Hedge Fund Compliance

CHAPTER 1

Introduction to Hedge Fund Compliance

INTRODUCTION

Nearly every profession, whether it is asset management, healthcare, construction, or scientific research, has some areas that require rules and regulations to be followed. At its most basic level, the term *compliance* refers to the processes and procedures by which an organization adheres to these guidelines. These guidelines may come from a variety of sources. Traditionally, the government is the primary initiator of compliance rules for different industries, but they may come from other sources as well.

Compliance has become a critically important component of investment management and this is particularly true in the hedge fund space. Key questions this book will seek to answer include:

- What exactly is hedge fund compliance?
- How can hedge funds design and improve their compliance function?
- What constitutes best practice compliance?
- What role do financial regulators play in implementing and monitoring compliance?
- Why should investors care about hedge fund compliance?
- What role can third-party service providers play in compliance?
- What global compliance trends are emerging in the hedge fund industry?

DIFFERENCES IN HEDGE FUND AND OTHER ALTERNATIVE FUND COMPLIANCE

Within the sphere of alternative investment fund managers, the lack of homogeneity creates a number of unique compliance challenges. Indeed, separate books could be written about the different compliance frameworks required to address the intricacies of different alternative asset classes, such as real estate and private equity.

Hedge funds, too, are unique from a compliance perspective. In particular, they tend to be one of the more complex fund management entities. Why? For starters, let us clarify what the term *hedge fund* refers to. **Hedge fund** is a broad umbrella term used to classify many different types of managers that may be organized under differing fund legal structures. The broad nature of the term is one of the reasons that make the category of fund managers known as hedge funds unique and challenging from a compliance perspective. Other key reasons for the increased complexity of hedge fund compliance include:

- *Variety of different strategies employed*—Hedge funds utilize a number of different investing strategies. Common hedge fund trading strategies include global macro; long-short equity; market neutral; event-driven strategies, including merger arbitrage and special situations; convertible arbitrage; sector funds, including healthcare or energy funds; quantitative strategies; and even multistrategy funds. Although other types of alternative investment categories contain distinctions, the variety of investment strategies employed by hedge funds is relatively large in comparison.

- *Trading and operating on a global scale*—In many cases, hedge funds may conduct not only trading but also fund-structuring and asset-raising activities in multiple jurisdictions around the globe. This global landscape contributes to the complexity of the compliance environment surrounding hedge funds.

- *Wide range of instrument types traded*—To facilitate both the trading activities of a wide number of strategies, as well as the broad investment flexibility within different strategies, hedge funds often trade a wide variety of instruments. These can include equities; swaps; swaptions; forwards; futures; options; various types of bonds, including treasuries, convertible bonds, and catastrophe bonds; bankruptcy claims; syndicated loans, including bank debt, mortgage-backed securities, private investments in public equity (PIPES), repos, and reverse repos; commercial mortgage-backed securities (CMBS); and credit default swaps (CDS). The use of different strategies can-not only subject hedge funds to the oversight of different financial regulators and exchanges but the combined effect of utilizing multiple instruments also increases the complexity of administering compliance across various security types.

■ *Variety of trading implementation strategies*—To implement trading strategies, hedge funds may employ a wide variety of trading procedures. These may include variations on:

i. Who is actually deciding to trade? (i.e., a human being, an automated computer trader, or some combination of the two)

ii. The timing of trades—Are they spaced into the market over time or all at once?

iii. The process of executing trades—Hedge funds may provide instructions to counterparties to execute trades in a number of different ways, including over the telephone or through electronic methods, such as instant message or e-mail. The reasons for this may depend on a number of factors, including the size of the hedge fund, the sophistication of a hedge fund's trading platform, the markets they trade in, and the way they work with trading counterparties. This variety presents a number of unique compliance challenges.

■ *Use of multiple prime brokers and other counterparties*—***Prime brokers*** are companies that facilitate the implementation of a hedge fund's trading strategy. Companies that provide prime brokerage services are typically referred to as ***broker-dealers***. In their work with hedge funds, they typically offer hedge funds a number of services, including trade clearing, execution, and leverage financing. Today, it is common for hedge funds to utilize multiple prime brokers.

Hedge funds do this for a variety of reasons, including diversifying their exposure across multiple counterparties as opposed to putting all of their eggs in one basket. The risk in using a single prime broker was highlighted after the 2008 failure of Lehman Brothers. There may also be other types of brokers utilized in addition to prime brokers. One example is brokers known as ***executing brokers***. These brokers typically work directly with prime brokers or, in some instances, directly with the funds, in executing trades. Another type of broker is called a ***futures commission merchant*** that facilitates trading in futures.

Hedge funds may also utilize a number of other trading counterparties for securities, such as swaps. These swap counterparties are commonly referred to in the industry as **ISDA counterparties**. This name comes from the standard master agreement often used to implement these arrangements that is provided by the the the International Swaps and Derivatives Association (ISDA).

The use of these multiple prime brokers and counterparties often creates unique needs among hedge funds for specific compliance oversight of the ways in which they interact with these groups.

■ *Enhanced research techniques*—From an investment research perspective, hedge funds traditionally employ a relatively wide array of techniques as compared to other fund managers. These avenues may include research activities, such as discussion with industry experts, and the utilization of *expert networks*. Expert networks are for-profit companies that organize databases of individuals with expertise in particular subjects or with particular companies. Expert networks then coordinate conversations between fund managers and these individuals in order to facilitate the fund manager's research. Accompanying the use of these research avenues are a series of additional layers of compliance oversight that would not otherwise be present in other alternative managers that do not engage in such techniques.

Each item listed above presents a specific set of compliance challenges that we will address in more detail throughout this book. The important takeaway at this stage is that, while there are certain core principles of compliance that can be applied across all asset classes, and within alternative investments in particular, based on the broad trading activities, strategies, and global scope of hedge funds, they present distinct compliance challenges that merit specialized compliance considerations.

HEDGE FUND COMPLIANCE IS NOT SPECIFIC TO ONE COUNTRY

Compliance is a heavily rules-based exercise. These rules are driven by the laws and regulations of the different countries in which hedge funds operate. Although we will address certain key aspects of different hedge fund regulations in the major countries in which hedge funds operate, this book is meant to provide practical compliance advice on a global basis rather than focus too heavily on the laws of any specific country. There are many other more technical resources that can provide in-depth specific guidance on the applicable compliance laws in any particular country.

Regional Compliance Expertise Used by Hedge Funds

In practice, many hedge funds engage in business activities in multiple countries. It is not practical for these hedge funds to maintain internal compliance experts who have expertise in all of the countries in which they may operate. To solve this problem, a hedge fund's interpretation and implementation of compliance guidelines in different countries often comes about as a result of consultation with a number of different country-specific specialists.

To clarify some terminology, individuals or firms that are not employees of the hedge fund but provide services to it are commonly referred to as *third parties*, *third-party firms*, or *service providers*. Although not every service provider provides compliance-related services to a hedge fund, many do in one form or another. One of the most common compliance-focused service providers is known as a *compliance consultant*. Another type of hedge fund service provider heavily involved in compliance is a *law firm*, which is also sometimes referred to as a hedge fund's *legal counsel*. The country-specific compliance specialists that hedge funds heavily rely on in the compliance area are typically either compliance consultants or legal counsel.

Another reason that many hedge funds utilize third-party compliance consultants when operating in different countries is because compliance is an evolving subject. As the laws and rules in different countries change, external expertise can often provide valuable insight into trends in compliance practices in specific countries.

Benefits to Developing a Global Understanding of Compliance

When studying the area of hedge fund compliance, there are benefits toward first establishing a general understanding of the subject on a global basis before delving too deeply into the rules of any one country. From the perspective of hedge fund employees, while individuals who are experts in the compliance practices of any single country are, of course, valuable, developing a global understanding of general compliance policies coupled with third-party country or region-specific compliance expertise as needed often produces a much more holistic compliance program.

From the perspective of hedge fund investors seeking to evaluate hedge fund compliance protocols, first developing a more general understanding of core hedge fund compliance principles prior to any country-specific knowledge is also advisable. This is because investors may allocate capital to hedge funds in multiple jurisdictions, which are subject to different compliance regimes. By developing this general compliance foundation first, which is then complemented by country-specific compliance knowledge, a more universal compliance due diligence program for investors will result.

Keeping both the hedge fund employee and the hedge fund investor perspectives in mind should assist you as you work through the material.

DO ALTERNATIVE INVESTMENTS MERIT SPECIAL COMPLIANCE CONSIDERATIONS?

Hedge funds are commonly grouped into an asset class known as *alternative investments*. Alternative investments differ from other types of investments, such as long-only mutual funds, commonly referred to as *traditional investments*. For reference, a *long-only fund* is one that only engages in the purchasing and selling of investments, such as buying or selling equities. These are long-only investments because the fund's general strategy is to make long-term predictions that the value of the investments will increase over time. Long-only funds do not follow a strategy of selecting investments by betting that the value of certain investments will decrease over time.

By contrast, an approach that seeks to profit from the decline in value of a potential investment, such as betting for a decline in the price of the shares of a publicly traded company, is known as *short selling*. Short selling is typically carried out through the use of equity options. One hedge fund strategy that combined both long- and short-selling techniques is known as a *long-short strategy*. In addition, other hedge fund strategies may also typically involve the use of options and other short-selling techniques. Other common types of alternative investments, often grouped alongside hedge funds in this category, are private equity, real estate, and commodity funds.

Within the area of fund manager compliance, the question may be raised whether alternative investment managers merit special compliance considerations as compared to traditional investment managers. When we refer to a *fund manager*, unless otherwise stated, we are not referring to a specific individual, such as a portfolio manager, but rather to the management company organization for which an individual known as a fund manager or portfolio manager typically works. Prior to answering the question of whether a special classification category is required for hedge funds, we must first understand the notion of market and regulatory classifications.

Contrasting Regulatory and Market Classifications

Most regulators have big categories by which they categorize similar types of financial entities. This is in contrast to the smaller distinctions among different types of asset managers that may be made in the real-world marketplace. When it comes to hedge funds, the majority of global financial regulations do not maintain a separate classification for entities that may be classified as a hedge fund, private equity fund, or any other alternative investment vehicle. Instead, within the broad umbrella of regulatory fund manager entities, financial regulations are primarily more driven by the activities of these fund managers. This concept highlights the distinction between what may be referred to as a *regulatory classification* and a *market classification* of a fund manager.

Understanding Regulatory Classifications A regulatory classification is the way a fund manager would be classified based on predetermined regulatory classification requirements. One way to think about regulatory classifications is the way in which a fund manager is viewed from a legal perspective.

For example, in the United States, if a fund manager under the *Investment Advisers Act of 1940* (Advisers Act, or Act) and accompanying statutes meets certain specific criteria, then the manager is classified as an entity known as an *Investment Adviser*. In general, Section 202(a)(11) of the Advisers Act defines an "Investment Adviser" as any person or firm that:

> *(1) for compensation; (2) is engaged in the business of; (3) providing advice, making recommendations, issuing reports, or furnishing analyses on securities.*[1]

As you can see by these general criteria, the requirements are quite broad. This means that whether an organization is a long-only mutual fund or a long-short hedge fund manager, from a regulatory perspective, they are both Investment Advisers.

If an organization does not meet each criterion and isn't exempt for some other reason, then the manager is generally not classified as an Investment Adviser. Why does this classification matter? If a fund manager is not an Investment Adviser, then it would generally not have to register with the U.S. Securities and Exchange Commission (SEC). More specifically, the compliance programs of a registered hedge fund may be distinctively different from an unregistered fund.

Understanding Market Classifications A market classification is the way a fund chooses to portray itself in the market. Alternatively, it can be the way a fund is classified, typically by investors, based on its actual trading activities. Obviously, it is not in a hedge fund manager's interest to misclassify their activities, but sometimes these two classifications are the same, and in some cases, there may be differences in classification methods, depending on the classification requirements in place.

Market classifications can be contrasted from regulation classification in two primary ways. First, under market classifications, there are no bright-line criteria determining what constitutes one classification type (i.e., a global macro hedge fund) from another (i.e., an event-driven hedge fund). For reference, a *global macro hedge fund* is a fund that follows a strategy of investing in macroeconomic themes, typically utilizing a wide variety of financial instruments on a global basis. An *event-driven hedge fund* follows a strategy of investing around the occurrence of certain events, such as corporate mergers or litigation.

Second, there are not necessarily any specific requirements, legal or otherwise, imposed on a manager for labeling themselves, or being labeled, under a market classification. This is in stark contrast to regulatory classification, which can have a material impact on the activities of a fund manager.

Example of Market and Regulatory Classification Differences. To make the distinction between regulatory and market classifications more concrete, let us consider an example. Consider a U.S.-based fund manager that chooses to promote itself to potential investors as a hedge fund. This would be the market classification from the hedge fund's perspective. A potential investor may take a look at the fund manager's actual, or planned, investment activities and instead classify the fund under a more detailed classification of a global macro hedge fund. This would be an example of how the market classifications can differ, or at least be more specific, between the fund itself and the investor.

As noted earlier, there is no specific regulatory classification for hedge funds, so the fund cannot have the same market and regulatory classification in this case. What would the regulatory classification be? If we focus on just U.S. regulatory classifications, and not any other jurisdictions, and it is a U.S.-based hedge fund that meets the SEC requirements outlined earlier, then its regulatory classification would be that of an Investment Adviser. As this example demonstrates, a hedge fund, therefore, can be correctly referred to as being in different market or regulatory categories, depending on the specific classification system in place.

When discussing hedge fund compliance, the regulatory classification is typically the driving force over market classifications, as regulatory classifications facilitate the heart of the compliance guidelines that a hedge fund must adhere to. However, it is important to understand the concept of market classification so that the appropriate distinctions can be made between the two classification systems.

Example of multiple regulatory classifications. In the previous example, we alluded to the fact that a hedge fund may have multiple regulatory classifications. One reason for this multiple regulatory classification system is because a hedge fund may be subject to multiple regulatory agencies. To be clear, these classifications may come within the same country or across multiple countries.

In some cases, this oversight is driven by a hedge fund's trading activities. For example, certain hedge funds may engage in the trading of a type of security known as *commodity futures*. A commodity future is a security that allows a hedge fund to speculate on the future price of commodities, such as lean hogs, coffee, cocoa, and copper. In the United States, if a hedge fund were to engage in futures transactions, they would be regulated by the joint efforts of two different regulators known as the National Futures Association (NFA) and Commodity Futures Trading Commission (CFTC). The NFA is a type of agency known as a self-regulatory organization (SRO), whereas the CFTC is a federal regulatory agency. SROs will be covered in more detail in Chapter 2.

As part of this oversight by the CFTC and the NFA, a hedge fund may have to register under special regulatory classifications similar to the SEC's Investment Adviser category. Common classifications under the CFTC and NFA regimes are for a fund manager to register as a *Commodity Trading Advisor* (CTA), a *Commodity Pool Operator* (CPO), or perhaps as both.

UNDERSTANDING THE HEDGE FUND COMPLIANCE FRAMEWORK

With an understanding of why hedge funds present unique compliance challenges, we can begin to introduce more specifics related to the way compliance is approached in hedge funds. To do this, we will first analyze the makeup of a hedge fund's compliance framework. This will be followed by an introduction of the hedge fund compliance function. Last, the key parties in a hedge fund's compliance framework will be discussed.

A hedge fund's compliance framework is not just the compliance function within the hedge fund itself. This is a common point of confusion among investors in particular. While certainly, the heavy lifting is performed by the compliance function, there are also other elements within the hedge fund that perform compliance-related functions. Furthermore, outside of the hedge fund, there are a number of service providers and counterparties that also perform compliance-related functions. This relationship is summarized in Exhibit 1.1.

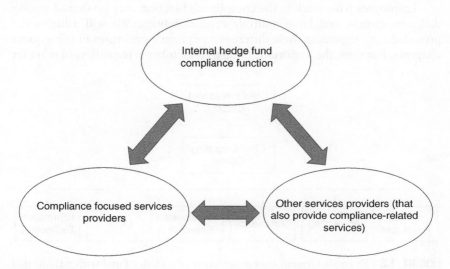

EXHIBIT 1.1 Components of a Common Hedge Fund Compliance Framework

Therefore, to fully understand the entire hedge fund compliance playing field, we must look beyond the compliance function within the hedge fund to analyze all of the key compliance stakeholders, both inside and outside the fund.

INTRODUCTION TO THE HEDGE FUND COMPLIANCE FUNCTION

The hedge fund *compliance function,* or *compliance department,* refers to a group within the hedge fund whose responsibility is to develop, implement, maintain, and test compliance policies and procedures. The compliance function often sits alongside other operational groups, such as fund accounting or technology.

One structure for a hedge fund compliance department is a *dedicated compliance function.* Under this structure, the compliance function only focuses on compliance-related tasks. This is in contrast to a *shared compliance function* structure, in which the compliance function may be combined with other departments within the hedge funds. A common structure for a hedge fund with a dedicated compliance function is outlined in Exhibit 1.2.

In a perfect world, every hedge fund would have enough resources to devote to developing a stand-alone dedicated compliance function (see Exhibit 1.2). In practice, for a number of reasons, including resource constraints, this is not always the case.

Employees who work in the compliance function may be shared among different groups and have multiple responsibilities. We will address the pros and cons regarding these different compliance structures in subsequent chapters. For now, the important thing to remember is regardless of whether

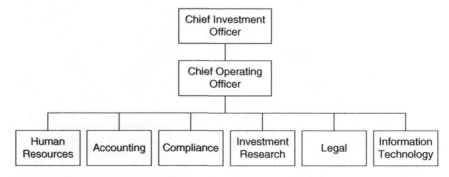

EXHIBIT 1.2 Example Organizational Structure of a Hedge Fund with a Dedicated Compliance Function

compliance department employees are shared, there will be individuals within the hedge fund who have a duty, in one form or another, to oversee compliance.

DISTINGUISHING THE LEGAL AND COMPLIANCE DEPARTMENTS

As Exhibit 1.2 demonstrates, a hedge fund may maintain both a legal and a compliance department. While these two departments may overlap with each other, they generally have different goals.

In other cases, a hedge fund may combine the legal and compliance functions into a single department. Reasons for this can include resource constraints on the hedge fund and a desire to centralize the responsibilities of certain individuals within the hedge fund. The two functions overlap to some extent, and combining them can represent a practical use of hedge fund personnel in certain instances.

The Legal Department Function

As can be expected, the legal function of a hedge fund is traditionally focused around tasks surrounding more legal, as opposed to compliance, matters. These legal tasks can cover a wide area. Common legal tasks performed by hedge funds typically include:

- *Traditional contract work*—Similar to many other businesses and fund managers, hedge funds engage in legal contracts, including employment contracts with senior personnel, rental agreements for office space, and vendor and service provider contracts. The legal tasks related to these contracts include drafting, reviewing, and negotiating contracts a hedge fund may enter into with a variety of parties.
- *Litigation management*—Hedge funds may sometimes be involved in lawsuits. These lawsuits may be initiated for a wide variety of reasons, including
  a. *Portfolio-related litigation*—Sometimes a hedge fund will initiate, or participate, in legal proceedings as part of the its investment strategy.
  b. *Employment related litigation*—Disputes may arise between a hedge fund and its employees, which includes direct employees of the fund as well as any consultants or other classes or individuals to which a hedge fund may maintain an employment obligation. These types of lawsuits can be broken up into two primary categories. The first category would be suits brought by the fund manager. The second would be those brought by employees.

- *Third-party law-firm management*—Hedge funds often work with third-party law firms to assist in a variety of legal matters, including those referenced earlier. A common internal legal task at a hedge fund is managing the work of these third-party firms.

Related but Not Equivalent

The legal and compliance functions of a hedge fund are often thought of as being related departments because a number of similarities exist between the two groups. There are several reasons for this, including

- Traditional shared coverage of both functions—The head of the legal function is commonly given the title of **General Counsel**, while the compliance function head is commonly referred to as the **Chief Compliance Officer**. Although not every hedge fund maintains a general counsel, historically the General Counsel at a hedge fund would have also maintained responsibilities for compliance-related functions. For example, it might not be uncommon for an individual with the title of General Counsel to also hold the title of Chief Compliance Officer.
- Shared basis in the law—Compliance and legal functions are both rooted in the law and legal principles; hence, the overlap among the functions.
- Complementary functions—The compliance and legal functions may be subject to oversight by each other in certain areas. For example, the activities of a hedge fund's legal department employees are typically subject to compliance oversight. Similarly, the development of compliance materials may require input from those with specialized legal expertise, which may come from the legal department.

So, while the hedge fund's legal and compliance functions overlap to a certain degree, the specific duties and goals are different—they are related but not equivalent.

KEY PLAYERS IN COMPLIANCE

A hedge fund's compliance efforts may be primarily driven by internal personnel. When this is the case, there are various individuals and groups that may be involved in the compliance function including those outlined below:

- *Chief Compliance Officer (CCO)*—The most prominent compliance professional is the Chief Compliance Officer. In addition to leading the compliance function, the CCO fulfills regulatory requirements.

Specifically, many regulators around the world require hedge funds to designate a CCO.

In addition, the CCO typically assists a hedge fund in complying with a number of other regulatory duties, including filing regulatory reports, developing compliance policies and managing daily compliance audit calendars. The CCO position is discussed in more detail in Chapter 3.

■ *Additional compliance personnel*—Similar to the CCO role, other compliance individuals may or may not be dedicated to compliance functions. Although the CCO position is mandated by regulators, other positions are not, and a fund may not have any other additional compliance employees. If this is the case, the CCO may perform all essential compliance functions themselves, or those tasks are outsourced, such as to a compliance consultant.

■ *Shared compliance employee*—A *shared compliance employee* is an individual who performs certain compliance duties in addition to other responsibilities outside of the compliance function.

Consider an example of a compliance department that is made up of six people, five of whom work solely on compliance-related tasks. The sixth person spends part of their time on compliance duties and the rest on noncompliance tasks, such as fund accounting. Under this structure, the compliance department may be referred to as either dedicated with supporting resources or a *mixed compliance department*.

■ *Noncompliance personnel*—Noncompliance personnel perform jobs in which compliance matters are not part of their daily activities. These individuals include everyone from investment professionals to fund accounting personnel. This does not mean they ignore the compliance function, but they do not focus on it as part of their regular duties.

■ *Compliance consultants*—Compliance consultants are third-party firms that provide advice on compliance-related matters to hedge funds. Their services range from completely running a hedge fund's compliance function to compliance policy development and assisting hedge funds with ongoing compliance management. It is not a requirement for hedge funds to maintain a compliance consultant, and not every hedge fund will have one. The roles of compliance consultants are discussed in more detail in Chapter 6.

■ *Other compliance-related service providers*—Other third-party service providers can focus more on supporting the infrastructure of the hedge fund, such as information technology consultants and utility companies. Although third-party service providers are not focused exclusively on compliance, they do perform compliance-related services. These other service providers are also discussed in more detail in Chapter 6.

STANDARD AREAS COVERED BY A HEDGE FUND COMPLIANCE FUNCTION

At this point in the reading, several basic compliance concepts have been introduced, and the structure of compliance departments has been discussed. We can now turn our attention to the key areas covered by compliance.

Standard Areas Covered by a Hedge Fund Compliance Function

At a very basic level, hedge fund compliance can be divided into two coverage areas: investment-related and non-investment-related compliance areas.

- Investment-related compliance areas. These areas directly relate to the investment management business of the hedge fund organization. Traditionally, this is where the majority of hedge fund compliance efforts are centered.

  Take, for example, trade allocation, in which a hedge fund manages two different funds that adhere to primarily the same investment strategy. Each fund has been created to accommodate the tax needs of different types of clients (onshore and offshore). When funds are managed in this structure they are said to be managed in what is known as a *pari passu manner*.[2] One fund is structured for clients who are typically based in the same country as the headquarters of the hedge fund. This is known as the *onshore fund*. The other fund is for investors based outside of the primary country in which the hedge fund operates. This is known as the *offshore fund*. Funds organized in this manner typically are structured to sit beneath what is known as a *master fund* that coordinates the underlying funds trading activities. In this structure, the onshore and offshore fund would be referred to as *feeder funds*, and the entire fund complex would be a *master-feeder structure*. Assume that our master fund makes a single purchase of 100 shares of Google stock. Typically, the stock would not remain at the master fund and would need to be allocated between the onshore and offshore feeder funds. But how should this allocation be completed? You might think it would be easiest to split the shares 50–50 among the two funds. Perhaps, however, the onshore fund contributed more of the capital to make the purchase happen and trade should be allocated in a method known as *pro-rata trade allocation*, which means that the trades should be allocated proportionally. Or what if the fund manager intended to buy more shares, or perhaps even all of the shares just for the onshore fund alone?

Alternatively, consider whether the performance of the offshore fund has been slightly worse as compared to the onshore fund. If this is a winning trade, then perhaps the fund manager would wish to boost the performance of this poor performing fund by allocating more shares to it. While benefiting the offshore investors, this would disadvantage the onshore investors.

It is the role of a hedge fund's compliance function to design the policies with regard to the way trades are allocated and to oversee the implementation of these policies in conjunction with investment personnel. In such an example, the compliance function would be tasked with playing an active role in overseeing that the allocation of trades among the funds is conducted in an manner that does not unfairly disadvantage the funds investors and complies with regulatory guidelines as well as the fund managers own internal policies.

- **Non-investment-related compliance areas.** These are areas where compliance policies and procedures relate to more operationally focused areas, such as guidelines and oversight governing the travel, gifts, and entertainment given to and received by the employees. A business development representative may travel to a conference to meet prospective clients. While this capital, if raised, will be utilized in the investment process, the actual travel and the raising of the capital does not directly relate to the day-to-day investments made by the fund. Therefore, it could be said that this type of compliance is in the non-investment-related compliance category.

Compliance plays a role in overseeing these types of activities. For example, if the prospective client is a government employee, there may be limits to the value of any gifts or meals they are allowed to receive. Similarly, to avoid gaining undue influence by service providers through lavish gifts, a hedge fund's own internal compliance policies may limit the value of gifts its own employees can receive.

- **Practical firm-wide compliance approaches.** In practice, the design of a successful hedge fund compliance management program does not place too much emphasis on the distinction between investment and operational compliance. Rather, the focus is on ensuring that all compliance policies and procedures, be they investment or noninvestment, are complied with. The distinction between the two is an important one to keep in mind however, from the perspective of implementing and managing the compliance function.

For example, consider a growing hedge fund undertaking an upgrade to its information technology, or IT, infrastructure. Although it is an operationally intensive project that may not necessarily be directly related to the investment work of the funds, certain aspects of investment-related systems, such as trading platforms used at the hedge fund, may change. Compliance oversight of this mostly operational project would likely need to keep in mind certain investment-related compliance requirements of the system upgrade. By keeping in mind the distinction and interrelatedness of operational noncompliance and compliance areas, a better design and management of the overall compliance infrastructure can be implemented.

This framework of the areas covered within the compliance function will be discussed in more detail in later chapters.

COMPLIANCE FUNCTION ROLES AND AUTHORITY

Compliance is a pervasive subject involved in all areas of the business of the hedge fund. The role and authority level of the compliance function, however, may differ, depending on the specific area of the hedge fund in question.

Although compliance dictates a majority of permissible and forbidden activities, there are many areas of a fund's activities that it may not necessarily address. Consider a hedge fund's management of fund expenses. There are few, if any, concrete regulatory guidelines about what constitutes an acceptable level of fund expenses. Similarly, there are a lack of guidelines about what actual expenses may be charged to the fund as long as hedge funds are transparent to their investors regarding what expenses are incurred. In practice, this is a decision typically made at the management level, and hedge funds often give themselves a large amount of leeway in setting their own expense guidelines. The compliance function, in conjunction with other service providers, such as auditors, are primarily focused on ensuring that the hedge fund does not violate its own policy in this regard rather than dictating what would be appropriate or best for the fund and its investors. In such circumstances, the job of the compliance function is often to serve as the enforcer of rules as opposed to an adviser helping to design them.

A related example would be an expense for a hedge fund that purchased a new computer server for its office. This server will be used by multiple departments within the firm for a wide variety of purposes, ranging from marketing and fund-raising for several different funds to storing data related to the investment management of a particular fund. Who decides what percentage of the cost of the server, if any, should be charged to a specific fund?

A hedge fund's own guidelines are likely to be vague and to provide management with a certain amount of discretion. So, if a manager decides to allocate 40 percent of the server to a single fund as compared to 30 percent, who is to say whether they are correct? In cases such as this, the decision about how much to charge a particular fund for the use of a server is often more of a business decision rather than a compliance one. The compliance function would oversee the choice that was made but not generally make the decision on the allocation.

As demonstrated by the expense management example above, when evaluating a compliance function, both hedge fund employees and investors should consider the flexibility afforded by policies. This type of analysis can help determine whether or not a fund's compliance program is designed too malleable, or rigid, to be effective.

CHAPTER SUMMARY

In this chapter, we began by outlining the concept that alternative investments merit special compliance consideration. We summarized the reasons that hedge funds are different from other types of alternative investments from a compliance perspective. Next, a distinction was made between market and regulatory compliance classifications. We then provided an introduction to the structure of compliance departments and distinguished between the legal and compliance functions. The key personnel and service providers that play a role in hedge funds compliance were then discussed. Finally, we provided an introduction to key investment and operational areas covered by compliance.

With this foundation in place, the next chapter will provide a more detailed overview of regulatory compliance with a focus on regulatory trends in popular hedge fund jurisdictions, including the United States and the United Kingdom.

NOTES

1. U.S. Securities and Exchange Commission. *General Information on the Regulation of Investment Advisers*, www.sec.gov/divisions/investment/iaregulation/memoia.htm.
2. Jason Scharfman, *Hedge Fund Operational Due Diligence: Understanding the Risks* (Hoboken, NJ: Wiley Finance, 2008).

CHAPTER 2

Introduction to Hedge Fund Regulation and Examination

INTRODUCTION

Society has an interest in ensuring that financial institutions, such as hedge funds, act in certain ways. This includes promoting what is deemed as good or acceptable behavior and discouraging or even punishing what is considered antisocietal or bad behavior. To further these goals, different countries, or groups of countries working together as may be the case in places such as Europe, have utilized their governmental and legislative authority to implement a structural framework to promote desired behaviors in hedge funds. This collective framework is known as *financial regulation*.

The laws, rules, and guidelines that make up financial regulations can be thought of as the rulebook by which a hedge fund must act to adhere to the law. If a hedge fund adheres to the required regulatory framework, then it can be said to be *in compliance*. Conversely, a hedge fund that operates outside of the financial regulations is *out of compliance*. For reference, financial regulation is primarily enforced by entities known as *financial regulators*. These entities will be discussed in more detail later in this chapter.

Regulation by itself also can be used to apply to the broad umbrella of regulations that are in place for multiple industries in addition to the financial space. The discussion throughout this book will use the terms *regulation* and *financial regulation* interchangeably for the simple reason that they are used that way in practice within the hedge fund industry.

DIFFERENT TYPES OF REGULATION FOR DIFFERENT FINANCIAL ENTITIES

Although our focus is on the financial regulation of hedge funds, it is important to remember that hedge funds interact with a wide variety of other types of financial institutions. Therefore, it is useful to understand the way financial regulation plays a part in overseeing these other financial entities, especially as it relates to their interactions with hedge funds.

Not every law, rule, and guideline in the financial regulation rulebook is universally applicable to every type of financial institution. This is because different types of financial institutions engage in different activities. For example, a hedge fund does not necessarily engage in the same activities as an insurance company or a bank and vice versa. To understand this, let us consider a financial service that many hedge funds deal with known as *prime brokerage*.

Prime brokers are a type of financial entity typically affiliated with banks. They offer a variety of services to fund managers of all types, including hedge funds. As it relates to hedge funds, the services are usually focused around facilitating their trading activities. Prime brokers may also lend stock to hedge funds to facilitate a fund's short-selling activities.

In other cases, a hedge fund may place assets with the prime broker to facilitate activities such as margin trading or as collateral for certain transactions. When placing assets with a prime broker, the broker then has the ability to lend those assets for other purposes for as long as it holds on to them. This is known as *rehypothecation* and is similar to the concept of a bank loaning out money it has on deposit from other people. When a prime broker rehypothecates assets, such as the securities of a hedge fund, it may use them for a variety of other purposes, including lending them to another hedge fund. Different jurisdictions maintain different rules regarding rehypothecation activities. Historically, in the United States, Rule 15c-3 of the Securities Exchange Act of 1934 limited the rehypothecation by the prime broker to 140 percent of the hedge fund's debit balance, while in the United Kingdom no such limits were in place.[1]

Unless it is a part of its investment strategy, a hedge fund does not participate in the lending and potential rehypothecating of securities in the same way a prime broker does. Therefore, regulations such as Rule 15c-3 do not directly apply to hedge funds in most cases.

Similarly, there are a host of activities a hedge fund may participate in that a prime broker would typically not, such as directly investing capital on behalf of its clients in securities. In these cases, there are regulations that apply to the hedge fund and not to the prime broker. As this example demonstrates, the universe of financial regulations can be quite broad and not every financial regulation applies to hedge funds. That being said, those in the hedge fund industry must still be familiar with the regulations that are applicable to the entities that a hedge fund may deal with such as prime brokers. The remainder of this chapter will focus on the specific regulations that apply to hedge funds directly.

WHY REGULATION IS NEEDED

Today, we may take for granted that hedge funds in the majority of countries are subject to some degree of regulation. This was not always the case, and there are any number of perspectives on the pros and cons of regulation.

Arguments against Hedge Fund Regulation

Common arguments against hedge fund regulation include:

- General antigovernment sentiments, including that government regulators are too involved in the financial industry
- Hedge funds have traditionally been investment vehicles for sophisticated investors who do not need the government to protect their financial interests
- Regulation of the hedge fund industry is best left to itself
- Regulation imposes too high of a cost of compliance on hedge funds and their investors by proxy

There are also criticisms raised regarding financial regulators. A common criticism is that regulators do not have the specialized knowledge or resources required to regulate the hedge fund industry sufficiently. Critics support this argument by pointing to a history of failures by regulators in not preventing fraud. One of the most notable recent examples is the failure of the U.S. Securities and Exchange Commission (SEC) to stop the multibillion-dollar Ponzi scheme perpetrated by Bernard Madoff.[2]

A related argument against hedge fund regulators is that in certain instances regulators have historically been ineffective because hedge funds had violated securities laws for years before being discovered. In addition to the Madoff case, another leading historical example of illegal activity going on for long periods of time undetected by regulators, is the insider trading case brought against hedge fund manager Raj Rajaratnam who founded one of the largest hedge funds in the world, The Galleon Group. It was alleged that Rajaratnam, along with others, had engaged in a long-term scheme of illegally exchanging and trading on insider information without detection from regulators.[3] Rajaratnam was eventually convicted of multiple crimes related to insider trading in 2009.[4]

Another common criticism of hedge fund regulation relates to the career aspirations of employees of financial regulators. The thinking goes that some of the individuals that work at financial regulators are building up a résumé of regulatory credentials in order to later monetize their regulatory experience by working at the very hedge funds they previously regulated. The argument continues that, even if the former regulatory employees do not go to work at a hedge fund, they will serve as consultants to them as to how to navigate around financial regulations, including how to deal with their former regulatory colleagues. Prior to turning himself into the government, Madoff highlighted this point, when discussing the SEC staffers, specifically saying, "These guys work for five years at the commission, then they become a compliance manager for a hedge fund now."[5] This revolving door of regulation results in what is known as a *captured regulator* because in essence the hedge fund industry being regulated has *captured* the regulator.

Arguments in Favor of Hedge Fund Regulation

On the other hand, common arguments in favor of hedge fund regulation include the following:

- Government oversight is required in order to adequately protect the larger financial system.
- Regulation helps protect investors by instituting minimum guidelines for investor protections.
- There is a public interest in government regulation of hedge funds as they increasingly manage more retail capital and capital for public and charitable institutions.[6]
- Regulation encourages increased transparency and record keeping.
- The ongoing threat of regulatory oversight minimizes future hedge fund violations.

Regulation Is Nonnegotiable

Historically, arguments against hedge fund regulation have held more weight for the simple reason that hedge funds were effectively unregulated for the vast majority of the early part of their existence. Over time sentiment towards regulation of the industry has changed, and today hedge fund regulation is commonplace worldwide. Reasons for this include:

- The 2008 global financial crisis, which resulted in a shift in attitudes toward enhanced regulation of the financial markets in general, and towards hedge funds in particular
- A series of fraudulent schemes, including the above referenced Madoff and Galleon cases
- Increased focus on the trading and tax avoidance practices of hedge funds
- More analysis on the ways in which hedge funds collect and utilize certain research data, including what may be deemed so-called

material nonpublic information (MNPI). MNPI is a legal concept by which certain information, which a hedge fund may collect or be exposed to due to its so-called insider nature, is illegal to trade upon. This is sometimes called *insider information.* Trading on this information is commonly referred to as *insider trading.* The rules surrounding MNPI vary from country to country. MNPI is discussed in more detail in Chapter 8.

The implementation and rigor of regulation varies around the world; however, once shunned practices, such as the registration of hedge funds with regulators in major jurisdictions in the United States and the United Kingdom, for example, are now commonplace.

WHERE DO COMPLIANCE RULES COME FROM?

A traditional approach to hedge fund compliance suggests an exercise that it is heavily rules-based. These regulations are usually rooted in legislation passed by governing bodies in different jurisdictions. In the United States, the legislative body would be the U.S. Congress. In the United Kingdom, it is Parliament. Once legislation is enacted, the rules are often further refined so they may be implemented in practice, and their enforcement is typically overseen by both the court system as well as governmental entities known as financial regulators.

Multiple Regulators in the Same Jurisdiction

Each jurisdiction does not necessarily have only a single financial regulator. In the United States, for example, a primary regulator of hedge fund activities is the SEC. As noted in Chapter 1, depending on the type of trading activities, hedge funds may also be subject to other financial regulators, such as the National Futures Association (NFA) and Commodity Futures Trading Commission (CFTC). In the United Kingdom, a single financial regulator, known as the Financial Conduct Authority (FCA), primarily oversees the activities of hedge funds within that country.

Self-Regulatory Organizations

In some cases, and depending on what country a hedge fund is located in, regulatory agencies may not be directly affiliated with the government but industry driven by quasi-governmental agencies. Such organizations are commonly known as *self-regulatory organizations (SRO)*. These are organizations of industry participants responsible for designing and enforcing rules for the industries they regulate. These rules are traditionally in line with broader laws from government financial regulators. In many cases, the actions of SROs are often overseen by financial regulators. The Financial Industry Regulatory Authority (FINRA) is the largest SRO in the United States, and the SEC is its financial regulator.[7] FINRA is responsible for regulating a wide variety of individuals and firms outside of the hedge fund industry as well as those within the industry in many cases.

Key Hedge Fund Regulators

Financial regulators in countries and in regions where clusters of hedge funds are located are influential in the global hedge funds regulatory construct. In the United States, key hedge fund financial regulators include the SEC, the CFTC, and the NFA. Financial regulators that oversee the work of hedge funds in Europe include the European Securities and Markets Authority (ESMA), the FCA, the Swiss Financial Market Supervisory Authority (FINMA), the Malta Financial Services Authority (MFSA). In Asia, key hedge fund regulators include the Hong Kong Securities and Futures Commission (SFC), the Japanese Financial Services Agency (FSA), and the Monetary Authority of Singapore (MAS). Finally, financial regulators in the Caribbean that oversee hedge funds include the Cayman Islands Monetary Authority (CIMA) and the Bermuda Monetary Authority (BMA).

NATIONAL AND GLOBAL JURISDICTION

The hedge fund industry is a global one; therefore, it is not unusual for a fund to operate in multiple countries. Similarly, it is also common for hedge funds to raise capital from investors all over the world. From a compliance perspective, these global activities can present regulators with a challenge.

Historically, the SEC would be focused on the activities of a hedge fund in the United States. If this same fund operated in the United Kingdom as well, the SEC would not have jurisdictional authority to regulate the fund's UK activities. Likely, the SEC would not have even been aware of the specific details or extent of the fund's activities in the United Kingdom. To correct this issue, regulators in major global jurisdictions have entered into cooperation agreements. For example, the SEC and regulators throughout the member states of the European Union and the European Economic Area, including the United Kingdom's FCA, have such an agreement in place. These agreements come in the form of a *memorandum of understanding*, the purpose of which is to better coordinate global regulatory efforts.[8] Similar arrangements have been in place for many years between the SEC, the CFTC, and Asian regulators, including the Hong Kong SFC.[9]

Regulator Funding

It is important to keep the ways in which these regulatory agencies are funded in mind as it can influence the regulatory priorities and the ways in which regulations may be implemented.

The ways in which regulatory entities are funded varies. The UK FCA, which is a governmental entity accountable to the UK Treasury and Parliament, does not receive funding from the government. Instead, it is funded through various fees, including filing fees, collected from the firms, including hedge funds, that it regulates.[10] This is similar to SROs, such as FINRA, which are also primarily funded by the fees it collects. It could be argued, as an extension of the captured regulator theory, that this fee model creates a potential conflict of interest, as the regulators may be inclined to levy less burdensome fines on the industry it has a financial interest in protecting. These industry funding fee models can be contrasted with government funding models. An example of this would be the SEC that is funded exclusively by the U.S. government.

Some argue that government-funded regulators should instead pursue a third model in which funding would be drawn not from the government or the entities it regulates, but from the fines collected from the firms it regulates. Some of those monies would be used to compensate the victims of violations.[11]

COMMON REGULATORY INTERACTION WITH HEDGE FUNDS

Regulators in different jurisdictions often have different types and frequency of interaction with the hedge funds they oversee. Regardless of these differences, there are a number of common goals regulators seek to accomplish when interacting directly with hedge funds including

- Information collection—To implement effective oversight, regulators need to collect various levels of information. The timing of this information collection may occur when a fund is first established or soon after it is launched. This information comes in a variety of different forms. One such method is reporting directly from the hedge funds themselves. This is known as *regulatory reporting*. Regulatory reporting is often coordinated by a hedge fund's Chief Compliance Officer (CCO). Regulatory reporting is discussed in more detail in Chapter 3.
- Ongoing monitoring—After initial information collection, regulators seek to collect further information on a periodic basis. This ongoing

monitoring is performed to ensure compliance with both external regulations and internal hedge fund guidelines.

■ Larger market risk assessments—In recent years, regulators have increasingly collected information from hedge funds to study larger market trends. This information is utilized for a number of different purposes, including to allow regulators to better monitor market liquidity and facilitate risk management assessments.

REGULATORY EXAMINATIONS

As part of their interaction with regulators, hedge funds subject to regulatory oversight are also often subject to examinations by these regulators. These examinations typically come in one of three common formats:

1. Routine examinations
2. Targeted and sweep inquiries
3. Regulatory reporting

Routine Examinations

The most traditional form of regulatory oversight is through *routine examinations*. These are reviews conducted by the regulator as part of their regular oversight. Traditionally, these reviews include an on-site visit by the regulator to the offices of the hedge fund.

Examination Schedules Regulators generally set a *regulatory audit schedule* as a way to organize their scheduling of routine examinations. The key features of regulatory audit schedules include:

■ *No required frequency for routine audits*—In general, regulators do not have a fixed frequency by which they must conduct routine examinations. While a specific regulator may have certain goals in mind with regard to the frequency they would like to routinely conduct examinations, it can change based on a number of factors, including shifting regulatory priorities and resource constraints. Timelines for routine examinations differ across regulatory jurisdictions.

■ *No scheduling transparency*—The specifics of the audit schedule are often maintained internally by the regulators on a confidential basis and are not shared with hedge funds. As a result, hedge funds generally do not know when their next routine examination will take place.

- *The number of examinations vary*—Certain hedge funds may undergo routine examinations more frequently than others. The reasons for this include:

    i. *Market risk evaluations*—Some regulatory agencies take the perspective that certain hedge funds pose more of a risk to the overall market in general and, therefore, should be reviewed with more frequency. Typically, this is the case in larger hedge funds in which their trading activities have the potential to have a larger impact on the overall health of financial markets.

    ii. *New lines of business or the launch of a new fund*—Hedge fund businesses are not static, and over time, a hedge fund may expand their operations. One way is by launching new funds. These new funds may adhere to completely different strategies or follow existing strategies. Individual funds that make up a hedge fund strategy are referred to as *vehicles*. New fund launches may draw the attention of regulators, which in turn may shorten the time in-between routine examinations. Alternatively, the launch of a new fund may trigger a regulator's attention to conduct a targeted or sweep exam (discussed later).

    iii. *Geographic considerations*—Depending on the available resources of the regulatory agency, hedge funds in different locations may be subject to different frequency of reviews. For example, one reason hedge funds in the tristate area of New York, New Jersey, and Connecticut may be reviewed more often than funds in other parts of the country, is because of traditionally higher staffing levels in this SEC office for these types of reviews. Of course, historically there has also been a greater concentration of hedge funds in this region as compared to the rest of the United States, which is one of the reasons for these traditionally relatively high staffing levels. However, by comparison, other SEC offices in the United States may not be as well resourced, in part because of the fewer firms operating in these other areas, and therefore, all else being equal, the hedge funds they regulate may not be reviewed as frequently.

The Chilling Effect and Bad Actor Principle The ambiguity of when routine examinations take place can create uncertainty among hedge funds. One of the benefits of examination scheduling ambiguity is that it creates what is known as a *chilling effect* on hedge funds compliance activities, especially those that may be in noncompliance with regulatory rules. Through this chilling effect, the threat of a routine examination has a potentially more powerful effect on ensuring that hedge fund activities remain in compliance with regulatory guidelines as opposed to an actual examination.

If we consider the limited frequency that routine examinations may take place, it becomes apparent why the chilling effect argument may hold merit. In the United States, for example, historically it was not unusual to come across a hedge fund that had not undergone a routine examination by the SEC for three years or more. Today, routine examinations are typically more frequent, as regulatory agencies have increased their examination focus and resources.

A popular contrary position to the chilling effect is the *bad actor principle*. Here, the argument goes that if a hedge fund manager is going to violate the law and skirt regulatory guidelines, they are going to do it regardless of when a regulator conducts a routine examination.

A second related contrary position is the notion that routine examinations can do nothing to detect past compliance violations. When there are periods of years between routine examinations, a hedge fund manager could simply continue with compliance violations for extended periods without the fear of a regulator appearance. Such an extended time period would perhaps give the manager enough time to correct or hide technical violations before the regulator could detect them during a routine examination.

A third contrary position to the chilling effect is that when there is a long span of time between routine examinations, hedge fund managers do not take the threat of regulatory action too seriously.

In today's environment the chilling effect argument has been strengthened through routine examinations that often occur with more frequency. These routine examinations are often complemented by targeted and sweep examinations, which further increase the frequency in which regulators interact with funds.

Targeted Examinations and Sweep Inquiries

In certain instances, a regulatory agency conducts a more focused review of a hedge fund's activities. These reviews are called *targeted examinations or sweep inquiries,* and seek to focus on a hedge fund's activities in specific areas. This is in contrast to a routine examination that casts a much broader net in its evaluation. One example of recent targeted regulatory focus is the ways in which hedge funds approach cybersecurity. As such, it is not uncommon for a regulator to conduct similarly focused targeted examinations across multiple hedge funds.

Similarly, a regulator may seek to focus on certain activities based on a specific suspicion of potentially illegal practices. In such circumstances, a regulator may not conduct an on-site examination but, instead, will submit a written request to a hedge fund seeking specific information. In many cases, a hedge fund simply replies to the regulator's request, and that is the end of the review. Should further information be required, the regulator will follow up directly with the hedge fund with requests for clarification.

Regulatory Reporting

Routine examinations, targeted examinations, and sweep inquiries are all instances in which a regulator proactively reaches out to a hedge fund to collect information. In most jurisdictions, hedge funds are also required to provide certain types of information to a regulator without a specific request. The timing of these filings varies based on a number of factors, including the assets under management of the hedge fund and the type of information being provided. This process is known as *regulatory reporting*.

Traditionally, a hedge fund's CCO is involved in overseeing the regulatory reporting process. This process is discussed in more detail in Chapter 3, which focuses on the duties of the CCO.

CHAPTER SUMMARY

We began our hedge fund regulation discussion by introducing core concepts related to the regulatory oversight of hedge funds. Next, we outlined the importance of the regulation of hedge fund service providers and counterparties. To demonstrate this, an example was given of the regulations surrounding the way a hedge fund's prime brokers may rehypothecate securities on loan from a fund. Arguments in favor of and against hedge fund regulation were then discussed, followed by an overview of key hedge fund financial regulators and the introduction of self-regulatory organizations. An overview of common regulatory interaction with hedge funds, including information collection and larger market risk assessments, was also introduced. Finally, we discussed the considerations surrounding the regulatory examinations of hedge funds by financial regulators.

With this background of hedge fund regulation and regulators, in the next chapter, we will address the person leading a hedge fund's interaction with regulators, the CCO.

NOTES

1. See Manmohan Singh and James Aitken, "Deleveraging after Lehman—Evidence from Reduced Rehypothecation," IMF Working Paper, March 2009.
2. See U.S. Securities and Exchange Commission Office of Investigations, "Investigation of Failure of the SEC to Uncover Bernard Madoff's Ponzi Scheme Public Version," Report No. OIG-509, August 31, 2009.

3. See A. Raghava, *The Billionaire's Apprentice: The Rise of the Indian-American Elite and the Fall of the Galleon Hedge Fund* (New York: Grand Central, 2013).
4. B. Lattman and A. Ahmed, "Hedge Fund Billionaire Is Guilty of Insider Trading," *DealBook*, May 22, 2011.
5. "Madoff, Caught on Tape, Reveals Ways to Dodge SEC," CNBC.com, September 10, 2009.
6. "Should Hedge Funds Be Regulated?," speech by SEC Commissioner Harvey J. Goldschmid, November 17, 2004, www.sec.gov/news/speech/spch111704hjg .htm.
7. "About FINRA," www.finra.org/about.
8. U.S. Securities and Exchange Commission, "SEC, European Regulatory Establish Supervisory Cooperation Arrangements Related to the Asset Management Industry," press release, July 19, 2013.
9. CFTC, "The CFTC, SEC and SFC of Hong Kong Sign MOU," press release, October 5, 1995, www.cftc.gov/opa/press95/opa3866-95.htm.
10. See FCA, "About the UK FCA," www.fca.org.uk/about.
11. See Dunstan Prial, "SEC: Self-Funding vs. Congressional Appropriations," FOXBusiness, May 17, 2013.

CHAPTER 3

The Chief Compliance Officer and Regulatory Reporting

INTRODUCTION

Chapter 1 provided a general introduction to the structure of a hedge fund compliance department, although it was emphasized that there is no one universal structure. Similarly, beyond minimum regulatory requirements, regulators across the globe do not mandate a specific compliance department structure. Regulators are instead, as discussed in Chapter 2, more focused on the actual compliance policies and procedures employed by funds.

INTRODUCING THE CHIEF COMPLIANCE OFFICER

Regardless of the structure of the compliance department, all compliance departments typically maintain an individual that holds the title of *Chief Compliance Officer* (CCO). The CCO is the leader of the compliance function and the nature of the position can come in many different forms, depending on the particular structure employed at the hedge fund. The more common CCO models include:

- *Dedicated* CCO—A hedge fund's CCO is focused solely on the compliance function.
- *Shared* CCO—In addition to the compliance function, the CCO has responsibilities outside of compliance, too.
- *Outsourced* CCO—A hedge fund may have a compliance structure whereby the CCO is not actually an in-house employee but a third-party individual who may work for themselves or as part of a larger firm.

Regardless of whether a CCO is in-house or outsourced, some of the compliance work may still be performed by third parties. The specific CCO model that is ultimately employed depends on the unique circumstances in place at each hedge fund.

Is a Chief Compliance Officer Required?

The compliance function of a hedge fund is a critical component of the firm's overall operations. Ensuring that compliance policies, procedures, and oversight are appropriately maintained, enforced, and updated requires someone to be responsible for overseeing the compliance function. Therefore, logically having an individual designated as a CCO makes good operational sense.

Not surprisingly, many regulatory agencies agree with this line of thinking and require hedge funds to maintain a CCO. For example, in the United States, Rule 206(4)-7 of the Investment Advisers Act of 1940 (Advisers Act) and Rule 38a-1 under the Investment Company Act of 1940 (Investment Company Act) require that hedge funds registered with the U.S. Securities and Exchange Commission (SEC), "designate an individual as CCO to be responsible for administering the policies and procedures" in place at a hedge fund.[1] Similarly, the UK's Financial Conduct Authority (FCA) maintains a regulatory category for a key individual involved in compliance, known as the so-called control functions with significant influence, under CF10 Compliance oversight function.[2]

The Role of the Chief Compliance Officer

Regardless whether a hedge fund's CCO is dedicated, shared, or outsourced, the industry, and most regulators as well, agree there are certain critical goals the role of the CCO should fulfill.

A central best practice in designing the CCO role is that they should have sufficient seniority and authority within the hedge fund to properly implement compliance protocols. The SEC's guidance outlines that Chief Compliance Officers should be "empowered with full responsibility and authority to develop and enforce appropriate policies and procedures."[3] A key element of this authority relates specifically to the seniority of the COO. The SEC's guidelines further outline that CCOs should maintain sufficient authority to "compel others to adhere to compliance policies and procedures."[4] The question becomes, then, how exactly is a hedge fund's Chief Compliance Officer supposed to execute these duties?

Promoting a Culture of Compliance

At a high level, the CCO seeks to promote what is commonly referred to as a *culture of compliance*. Although this is not a technical legal term, most hedge funds express their desire to establish such a compliance culture, but what exactly does it mean? The definition is not necessarily clear-cut.

Most regulators and hedge funds agree that a critical element toward establishing a compliance culture is for the CCO to administer a framework that ensures the fund complies with all regulatory rules and guidelines. However, this type of compliance is certainly not what many would refer to as best practice compliance but rather, simply minimal compliance. Instead, a culture of compliance seeks to impart the notion that a hedge fund not just meets minimum regulatory requirements but also exceeds them. In this way, the role of a CCO is to not only tick the box of strict compliance but also to serve in an aspirational role to promote best practice compliance oversight throughout the firm.

CCO Qualifications

A common question that arises about the position of CCO is whether specific qualifications are required to be one. From a regulatory perspective, the SEC's guidelines state that a hedge fund's CCO should be "competent and knowledgeable."

Although these are admirable goals, they are also vague and hedge funds grapple with what "competent and knowledgeable" actually means in practice. CCOs generally are not required to have any special education, training, or compliance experience to be named to the position. This means, for example, that an individual who has training as an accountant and has never worked in any aspect of compliance could hold the CCO title at a hedge fund. Why would this be allowed? Wouldn't some experience with compliance make sense? To understand the vagueness behind the guidelines, it is helpful to frame the development of the CCO role in the hedge fund industry.

Historically, particularly in many smaller hedge funds, the CCO role was viewed by many as ceremonial in nature, with the heavy lifting of compliance often performed by third-party groups, such as a firm's legal counsel. As an extension of this, the CCO would often have another primary job such as Chief Financial Officer or Chief Operating Officer. Alternatively, as discussed in Chapter 1, if a hedge fund was large enough to maintain a dedicated individual responsible for the legal function (General Counsel), that individual may have shared the CCO role as well. The fact that the CCO role was often filled by individuals with multiple titles likely contributed to the development of vague regulatory guidelines on CCO qualifications. The regulators likely did not want to create a disconnect between required CCO qualifications that were too strict and the actual practices that were in place at hedge funds of having individuals in multiple roles and with noncompliance backgrounds acting as CCOs. Today, a different trend has emerged, particularly in larger hedge funds, where CCOs often have specialized legal and compliance backgrounds. Indeed, as the hedge fund industry has matured, today's CCO may have extensive experience in compliance or may have even previously worked at financial regulators.

In smaller hedge funds, it is sometimes not feasible for a firm to employ a dedicated CCO. In those cases, a shared CCO with a limited compliance background coupled with sufficient outsourced compliance support resources may be an appropriate compromise. This type of structure would typically still employ an in-house employee with the CCO title, as opposed to an entirely outsourced CCO structure.

CCO Duties

While there are a certain core set of compliance duties that every hedge fund CCO must perform, in practice the specific tasks and volume of work varies among hedge funds based on a number of factors. The size of the hedge fund often influences the level or activity and specific duties of the CCO. For example, a hedge fund with 500 employees will have more practical compliance challenges in place than a hedge fund with five employees.

Another influencing factor is the *regulatory complexity* of a hedge fund's investment activities. This is the amount of regulatory oversight applied to different hedge fund strategies. For example, consider an equity hedge fund that follows a long-short investment strategy that does not have a high *trading volume* and conducts fewer than 50 trades a month. Compare this to a different hedge fund that follows a *high frequency trading (HFT) strategy* and executes high volumes of trades. Software programs, subject to oversight by humans, typically manage the large volume and speed by which HFT trades are executed. From a compliance perspective, the larger volume of trading presents a greater set of activity to be monitored by the CCO. Therefore, an HFT strategy has a greater degree of regulatory complexity as compared to the more straightforward long-short strategy. Of course, this does not mean that the long-short manager may not also present regulatory and compliance challenges; however, from the perspective of the volume of trades alone, a CCO at an HFT manager would have more compliance work in this area.

At its most basic level, the role of a hedge fund's CCO is to lead the compliance function. What does that mean exactly? There are a number of common tasks expected of the compliance function. They include:

- Compliance training
- Compliance testing
- Compliance policy maintenance and new policy development
- Company secretarial services for committees
- Managing the work of compliance consultants

The level of CCO involvement in these tasks varies. In a smaller hedge fund, the CCO may be the sole compliance employee and perform all compliance tasks. In a larger hedge fund, the day-to-day compliance work may be performed by other compliance personnel or outsourced to third parties, and the CCO oversees the work of these individuals in a mostly managerial capacity.

As we noted in previous chapters, a key compliance task traditionally overseen by the CCO is managing the reporting made to financial regulators.

REGULATORY REPORTING

As introduced in Chapter 2, an area of increasing responsibility for hedge funds is regulatory reporting. Routine examinations, targeted examinations, and sweep inquiries are all instances in which a regulator proactively reaches out to a hedge fund to collect information. In most jurisdictions, hedge funds are also required to take the initiative to provide information to regulatory agencies without a specific request. This is known as *regulatory reporting*.

Depending on a number of factors, including the CCO's background and familiarity with the regulatory requests and forms, as well as the resources of the hedge fund, the level of involvement of the CCO may vary. For example, the CCO could be the one to collect the required data and complete the regulatory forms. Alternatively, the CCO could instead review the work of those who collect this data and prepare the filings. Typically, as the lead compliance professional, the CCO serves as the key point of contact for questions or requests for additional information regulators may have regarding the reporting. In certain instances, a hedge fund's CCO may also be required to sign the filings. The thought process being that if the CCO is required to attest to the information's accuracy and, in turn, has subsequent liability associated with these attestations, they will be incentivized to ensure it is properly reported.

REGULATORY REPORTING IN MULTIPLE JURISDICTIONS

A hedge fund may be required to file regulatory reporting in multiple jurisdictions. Consider, for example, a hedge fund headquartered in the United Kingdom that also conducts business in the United States. Depending on the nature of the hedge fund's activities, it may be required to report information to regulators in both the UK and the United States.

A UK-based CCO may be familiar with UK regulatory reporting requirements but less familiar with the intricacies of U.S. reporting requirements. In these instances, the CCO's level of involvement with the U.S. reporting process will likely be different as compared to the UK filings. In such a case, many hedge funds will work with a U.S.-based third-party service provider, such as a law firm or a compliance consultant, to assist with the filings.

COMMON REGULATORY REPORTING QUESTIONS

When it comes to regulatory reporting, a hedge fund manager and its compliance employees often wants clear answers to the following questions:

- Which reports do I need to file?
- When do I need to file them?
- How often do I have to file them?
- When do I have to make additional filings?

The compliance rules regarding regulatory reporting can be quite complex. Straightforward answers to these questions often require an analysis of each hedge fund's specific circumstances and the specific requirements of each different applicable financial regulator. As the subsequent examples relating to Form ADV will demonstrate, it is not practical to provide detailed responses to these questions for every manager scenario here. Instead the goal in this reading is to focus on the general process by which a hedge fund would approach these questions.

In practice, specific expertise with each regulator is often required to facilitate the regulatory reporting process. This is why many hedge funds employ not only in-house legal and compliance personnel to analyze the issues raised by the above referenced reporting questions but also utilize third-party compliance consultants and external legal counsel to provide guidance. In some cases, other service providers, such as hedge fund administrators, may be involved in the regulatory reporting process also.

A MULTISTEP PROCESS

Regulatory reporting is a multistep process of providing information to hedge fund financial regulators. On a high level, the steps in the reporting process are:

Step 1: Evaluate a hedge fund's regulatory reporting eligibility requirements.
Step 2: Determine what specific forms and data are required.
Step 3: Develop a strategy regarding what data to provide.

Step 4: Select the appropriate method and group to transmit information
to a regulator.
Step 5: Adhere to ongoing filing requirements.
Step 6: Conduct ongoing evaluations of new filing requirements.

Step 1: Evaluate a Hedge Fund's Regulatory Reporting Eligibility Requirements

A hedge fund must first determine whether it is under the jurisdiction of a particular regulator for filing purposes.

Consider a U.S.-headquartered hedge fund with a one-person client service office in the United Kingdom. Is this hedge fund required to make any regulatory filings with the United Kingdom's regulator, the FCA? Likely not, because it is not managing any client funds in the UK but, rather, is simply conducting client outreach and servicing.

Let's make the scenario more complex. What if the UK office has both a client service professional and a single trader? Regulatory reporting is likely required because trading activities are conducted in the office, which would also likely trigger a UK FCA registration requirement.

There are any number of scenarios to consider. What if the UK office has a client service employee and a second employee with a nontrading role who assists U.S.-based traders in processing trades? What if someone conducts investment research in Europe, including the UK, but does no trading from the UK office? Do the regulatory reporting requirements change? The various iterations of scenarios present unique situations for hedge funds that require individualized evaluations as to whether regulatory reporting is required.

Regulatory Reporting Does Not Always Imply Regulator Registration It may seem intuitive that if a hedge fund has gone through the first step in the process and determined it is required to make certain filings with a regulator, that the hedge fund must have first been required to be registered with that regulator. In fact, it is not always the case that hedge fund registration goes hand in hand with filing obligations. In certain circumstances, based on factors such as the nature of a fund's trading activity, a hedge fund may not be required to register with a regulatory agency but still may be required to make filings.

Step 2: Determine What Specific Forms and Data Are Required

Once a hedge fund has determined that it is indeed required to make filings with a regulator, what data must be provided and what forms are needed?

As is often the case within compliance, the answer depends on the specific circumstances of each hedge fund. Elements including a fund's assets under management and the type of securities traded will influence reporting decisions. Even factors such as the volume of trades may determine whether certain regulatory reports have to be filed. For example, the Large Trader Data reporting requirements of the U.S. Commodity Futures Trading Commission (CFTC) implements enhanced reporting requirements for funds that engage in trading above certain predetermined trading volume thresholds.[5]

Hedge funds typically adhere to particular investment and trading strategies. While there are differences among fund managers, the broad characteristics of managers within strategies do not generally differ radically from a compliance perspective. Those familiar with the regulatory reporting process can often provide initial guidance based primarily on familiarity with certain groups of strategies. For example, two different hedge funds that follow the same general strategy, but are different in their implementation, in many instances would likely be required to make the same core regulatory filings in the same jurisdiction. Likewise, a hedge fund with multiple strategies will have different filing requirements with different regulators across for each strategy type.

Step 3: Develop a Strategy Regarding What Data to Provide

It is a common misconception that regulatory reporting and data provision is a rote, straightforward, rules-based exercise. This is not the case for several reasons.

- Special technical definitions of regulatory data points. The definitions of commonly requested data points in the regulatory reporting process is not always straightforward, and may not have the same meaning across different filings. For example, if a fund is asked to provide assets under management (AUM) to an investor based on U.S. Generally Accepted Accounting Principles (GAAP), the figure that is typically provided is the sum total of the assets of each of the firm's different funds on a net basis. However, SEC Form ADV and Form PF ask instead for *regulatory assets under management* (RAUM), which reflects gross assets without subtracting debt or leverage.[6] RAUM figures tend to make a hedge fund appear larger than they are.
- The interpretation of regulatory guidelines can influence the scope of filings. Continuing the RAUM example, there are assumptions a hedge fund is required to make when calculating this figure. Two examples of areas where these estimates come into play is when a hedge fund makes its leverage calculations and aggregates data across multiple funds.

The way these assumptions are made may vary among hedge fund managers. This was particularly true when RAUM calculations were first introduced in 2012. This was because first-time filers were unsure of what regulators considered reasonable assumptions. As a result, the details in RAUM filings varied significantly among funds.

Why do figures like RAUM matter? For starters, no manager wants to intentionally mislead regulators or deviate radically from common industry wisdom about how to appropriately interpret regulatory data requests. Equally important, figures such as RAUM directly influence the scope of regulatory filings. Under SEC Form PF, for example, a hedge fund's RAUM calculation determines which sections of the form must be completed and how frequently it must be updated. Conservative RAUM estimates may fall below a predetermined threshold, which result in less frequent filings. Conversely, less conservative assumptions result in overreporting RAUM and unnecessary overfilings.

- **Concerns about misinterpretation of data by different parties.** Hedge fund managers may have concerns that data reported to regulators in a specific requested format could be misinterpreted by parties for which the reporting was not originally intended.

Continuing the RAUM example, the calculation methodology required by the SEC makes it not uncommon for RAUM to be higher than GAAP's AUM, which as noted above is the figure commonly provided to investors. These differences can lead to confusion among investors who may not be educated in the specifics of RAUM calculations or unfamiliar with the assumptions made in calculating RAUM. As a result, hedge funds want to avoid these types of situations and may wish to not share certain regulatory reporting with investors. In certain cases, regulators are sensitive to these types of issues and do not make certain filings, including Form PF, available to the public. Nor is there a requirement that a hedge fund is required to release certain filings to investors or prospective investors, even if it is requested. As a compromise, many hedge funds provide partial filings to investors on request and often highlight the assumptions used in making the filings. While these approaches do not influence how a manager completes a particular regulatory request, they do influence the way in which data may be shared with investors.

- **Estimated data may change over time.** A hedge fund may be required to make certain estimates with regard to items that have not been finalized at the time of regulatory reporting.

For example, on Form PF a hedge fund manager is required to make a good faith estimate regarding potential investor *redemptions* likely be to be triggered during conditions of significant market stress.[7] A redemption is when an investor submits notice to a hedge fund that it would like to withdraw capital from the fund. Due to the fact that an investor may see some portion of this regulatory filing, it is not unreasonable to see why a hedge fund may wish not to overestimate the likely volume of potential withdrawals in the event of market stresses. Therefore, how to best determine such estimations requires discretion and strategy by the hedge fund to address both the direct, intended audience—the regulators—as well as secondary audiences—investors.

Step 4: Select the Appropriate Method and Group to Transmit Information to a Regulator

Regulators have differing requirements for how information must be submitted, and hedge funds must comply with these rules. Common submission formats include:

- *Web-based regulatory systems*—Many regulators utilize web-based systems to facilitate regulatory filings. Such a format can include special forms on their websites. Common web-based systems include:
  - SEC Investment Adviser Registration Depository (IARD) website: www.iard.com
  - Cayman Islands Monetary Authority (CIMA) Regulatory Enhanced Electronic Forms (REEF): reefs.cimaconnect.com
  - The United Kingdom Financial Conduct Authority (FCA) GABRIEL: www.fca.org.uk/firms/systems-reporting/gabriel
- *E-mail filings*—Certain regulatory forms, or questions regarding clarification on forms, are transmitted via e-mail. For example, see the UK FCA's "Where to submit your returns" guidelines at www.fca.org.uk/firms/systems-reporting/where-to-submit-your-returns

Additionally, the format of data submitted through websites or e-mail may be subject to certain restrictions or considerations unique to the regulator. For example, hedge funds can submit their Form PF filings in an electronic file format called XML, a coded format that makes the information readable by either humans or machines.

Who actually prepares and submits the regulators' filings? In certain instances, a hedge fund will work with an external service provider, such as legal counsel or a compliance consultant, to perform these tasks. Depending on factors including the level of complexity of the filings, the frequency of filings required, and the internal compliance resources in place at the hedge fund, it may be more efficient to leverage on service providers, to support the filings process. As a reminder, just because a third-party group is utilized to assist in preparing the filings does not remove the requirement to have the CCO involved. Ultimately, the CCO is responsible for the filings and, in some cases, actually signs them.

Step 5: Adhere to Ongoing Filing Requirements

Once initial filings are completed, there is often a requirement to update the forms and information provided. The frequency of updates depends on a number of different factors. Certain regulatory forms, for example, have a predetermined frequency, such as annually, for when information must be updated. The size of the figures such as the reported regulatory assets under management also influences the frequency of updating information. As stated earlier, the SEC's Form PF has more frequent filing requirements for larger hedge funds.

Step 6: Conduct Ongoing Evaluations of New Filing Requirements

When a hedge fund enters into certain types of new investing activities, previously filed forms may require updating or entirely new forms may need to be filed. Depending on the nature of these new activities, a hedge fund may be subjected to further regulatory scrutiny as well. A common example would be a hedge fund that launches an affiliated broker-dealer entity to facilitate the marketing of its funds. In the United States, this entity would traditionally be subjected to additional oversight by FINRA.[8]

CHAPTER SUMMARY

In this chapter, we focused on the role of the CCO. We first introduced the three common CCO models: dedicated, shared, and outsourced. Next, we discussed considerations relating to the CCO's role in promoting a culture of compliance. The technical requirements to maintain a CCO role, as well as the absence of specific regulatory mandated requirements for CCOs was also addressed. The common tasks of hedge fund compliance departments and the CCO's efforts in those areas was also discussed. Finally, we analyzed the six steps of the regulatory reporting process and the CCO's role in it.

With the role of the CCO now established, the next chapter will focus on the role of other compliance professionals and mechanisms.

NOTES

1. See National Exam Program Risk Alert, "Examination of Adviser and Funds That Outsource Their Chief Compliance Officers," vol. 5, no. 1 (November 9, 2015).
2. Financial Conduct Authority, "Controlled Functions," May 12, 2015.
3. U.S. Securities and Exchange Commission, "Final Rule: Compliance Programs of Investment Companies and Investment Advisers," www.sec.gov/rules/final/ia-2204.htm.
4. Ibid.
5. U.S. Commodity Futures Trading Commission, "Large Trader Reporting Program," press release, www.cftc.gov/IndustryOversight/MarketSurveillance/LargeTraderReportingProgram/index.htm.
6. See M. Celarier, "Leverage Isn't What It Used to Be," *Alpha*, June 1, 2012.
7. See U.S. Securities and Exchange Commission, "Form PF," paper version, www.sec.gov/about/forms/formpf.pdf.
8. See FINRA, "Register a New Broker-Dealer Firm," www.finra.org/industry/new-bd-firm-registration.

CHAPTER 4

In-House Compliance Professionals and Hedge Fund Committees

INTRODUCTION

As outlined in Chapter 1, the resources that make up a hedge fund's compliance function can come from one or both of two primary sources. The first set of resources comes from outside the hedge fund. These are commonly third-party compliance consultants and legal counsel. Other service providers, such as fund administrators, auditors, and prime brokers, also contribute to compliance implementation.

The second source of compliance resources, and the one that is the focus of this chapter, comes from within the hedge fund. In addition to the Chief Compliance Office (CCO), a hedge fund may also employ other individuals to varying degrees in implementing the compliance function. Just as with CCO models, there are three distinct groups of compliance professionals:

- *Dedicated compliance employees.* They are solely focused on compliance tasks and supporting the work of the CCO. Depending on their seniority and the structure of the department they may have titles, such as Compliance Associate and Deputy Compliance Officer.
- *Shared compliance employees.* These employees spend a certain percentage of their time on compliance-related duties but also maintain roles outside of the compliance function. The percentage of time spent on compliance duties is not necessarily fixed and may vary based on the demands placed on the employee's time.
- *Noncompliance personnel.* These employees have primary tasks not directly related to compliance but may still be involved in aspects of compliance as part of their daily duties. For example, a hedge fund trader is partly responsible for ensuring trades do not violate predetermined compliance policies of the firm.

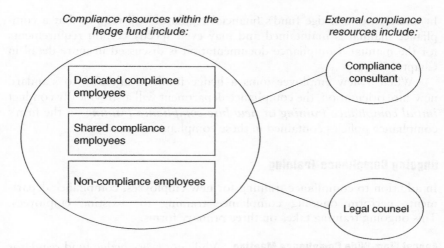

EXHIBIT 4.1   Example Structure of Internal and External Hedge Fund Compliance Resources

When categorized together this larger group of dedicated and shared compliance employees can be referred to as *in-house compliance professionals*. Exhibit 4.1 shows an example of the structuring of internal and external compliance resources.

COMMON COMPLIANCE FUNCTION TASKS

The CCO of a hedge fund can be thought of as a military general leading a division of troops. Generals are rarely directly on the front lines but rather establish strategy and oversee the implementation of that strategy. At a high level this is the role of the CCO. In a well-resourced hedge fund the in-house compliance professionals, and perhaps service providers, perform the heavy lifting of day-to-day compliance tasks subject to oversight of the CCO. As noted above, depending on the scope of compliance resources available, the CCO may also pitch in on the day-to-day compliance tasks as well; however, a key component of their job is also managing the overall compliance function. Two common core compliance tasks that are elements of all compliance functions are compliance training and testing.

Compliance Training

Every hedge fund has compliance policies and procedures. These are typically codified in documents such as a *compliance manual* and *code of ethics*.

In many cases a hedge fund's financial regulator will require that a compliance manual is maintained and may even specify certain requirements for the manual. Compliance documentation is discussed in more detail in Chapter 7.

When a new employee joins a hedge fund, in addition to standard new-hire orientation, the compliance department will also typically conduct *initial compliance training* or *new hire compliance training* on the firm's compliance policies contained in these compliance documents.

Ongoing Compliance Training

In addition to compliance training for new employees, compliance departments perform ongoing compliance training for existing employees. This ongoing training takes on three primary forms.

Annual Firm-Wide Compliance Meeting   While not every hedge fund regulator may specifically mandate annual training, such meetings are encouraged and a regulator may inquire about the frequency and depth of employee compliance policy and procedure training during their examinations of a hedge fund. Therefore, conducting annual training as part of larger compliance training efforts is considered a best practice. Key features of this meeting include:

- *Meeting attendance and agenda development*—It is advisable for attendance to be taken at these annual mandatory meetings. Furthermore, a meeting agenda should be developed and distributed prior to the meeting. Such measures create a record for the hedge fund to use in analyzing its compliance training efforts on a year-over-year basis. It also creates documentation should a regulator inquire as to the details of a hedge fund's annual training meeting.
- *Meeting led by CCO or third party*—Either the Chief Compliance Officer or a third-party service provider, such as a compliance consultant or law firm, typically lead the annual training meeting.
- *Virtual participation*—If a hedge fund has multiple offices in different locations, it may be more cost efficient to conduct the annual meeting in person for the bulk of the firm's employees and allow other employees to participate in the meeting virtually via conference call or video conference.
- *Recap of compliance policies and procedures*—The annual meeting should include an overview of the firm's compliance policies and procedures. This provides employees an opportunity to refamiliarize themselves with compliance policies.

- *Updates on compliance changes*—Changes to compliance policies implemented in the past year are discussed at the annual meeting.
- *Updates on compliance trends and anticipated changes*—The annual meeting is an opportunity to provide an update on emerging compliance issues as well as introduce anticipated compliance changes that may be implemented in the coming year.
- *Question and answer session*—The annual compliance meeting also affords employees the opportunity to ask any questions regarding compliance matters.

Annual training meetings are also an opportunity to collect what are known as *employee acknowledgments.* These acknowledgments are typically mandated by hedge fund regulators as well as a hedge fund's own internal policies. Employee acknowledgments are compliance forms employees are required to complete acknowledging they have received the firm's compliance policies and procedures.

As either part of the acknowledgment form or as a separate form, employees are also typically tasked with affirmatively stating that they have complied with the hedge fund's compliance policies over the last reporting period. This is referred to as a *compliance attestation*, because the employees are attesting (i.e., affirmatively stating) that they have complied with the policies. Exhibit 4.2 is an example of a combined acknowledgment and attestation form.

In certain instances, employees may complete multiple additional acknowledgment and attestation forms to demonstrate adherence to specific compliance policies, such as the firm's code of ethics. Another example would be an acknowledgment that an employee has agreed to adhere to a hedge fund's policies relating to the protection of investor data. An employee may also need to attest that they have complied with a hedge fund's personal securities transaction policies, including the disclosure of any covered employee securities transactions throughout the reporting period. Compliance oversight of employee personal account trading is discussed in more detail in Chapter 6.

Employees are typically asked to complete these acknowledgments and attestations on at least an annual basis, if not more frequently, which is why it is convenient to time their collection around the annual compliance meeting. Some firms require signed hard copies while others accept electronic signatures.

Department-Specific Training In addition to annual firm-wide compliance training, a hedge fund may conduct more focused training for different departments. The purpose of these sessions is to focus on more granular

Acknowledgment Form for Compliance Manual of Sample Hedge Fund

By affixing my signature in the indicated areas that follow, I certify that I have received this compliance manual. I further certify that I have fully read and understood the material contained in this manual. Additionally, I acknowledge that I have fully abided by this manual and will continue to do so.

I also acknowledge that I understand that should I have any questions about this compliance manual I should directed them to the Chief Compliance Officer.

Print: _____

Signature: _____

Date: _____

EXHIBIT 4.2 Example Compliance Manual Acknowledgment for Hedge Fund Employee

compliance-specific rules that may be more applicable to certain job functions as compared to others.

For example, in March 2015, Swiss law was revised to require hedge funds outside of Switzerland to appoint a Swiss legal representative to serve as the fund's primary representative with the Swiss regulator FINMA.[1] In addition, as part of the revision in the law, these non-Swiss hedge funds were also required to appoint an entity know as a *paying agent*. A paying agent is effectively a bank, which would process investor subscriptions and redemptions.

An employee involved in servicing or raising capital from clients in Switzerland would need to be well versed in these rules, and specific compliance training in this area would be quite helpful. Such specific compliance training however, would not be as relevant for an investment professional who does not deal directly with clients, particularly those in Switzerland.

There is no harm in having the compliance department to make the entire firm aware of the general rules surrounding client service and business development compliance issues. Instead, the important point we are making here is that in addition to firm-wide training, different departments can benefit from receiving specific training geared toward the compliance challenges they will likely face in their daily jobs.

Issue-Specific Training Depending on the nature and importance of the particular area in question, issue-specific compliance training may be offered either on a firm-wide or departmental basis. If offered firm-wide, it could be bundled into the annual firm-wide training that would already be taking place. However, in practice, issue-specific training tends to delve into more detail than would be appropriate to cover in a larger firm-wide training session, so breakout issue-specific training sessions are preferred. The same holds true for issue-specific training on a departmental basis as well, where a stand-alone deep-dive into the specific issues are preferable to a more broadly focused departmental session.

A common example of an area that hedge funds conduct issue-specific training on is the compliance rules surrounding *material nonpublic information* (MNPI), sometimes called *insider information*, and the associated practice of trading on MNPI, commonly called *insider trading*. In recent years, there have been a continual stream of insider trading–related inquiries and enforcement actions brought by regulators. As such, hedge fund compliance departments have frequently conducted specific training sessions on this issue.

Compliance Testing

Compliance testing is the process by which the implementation and efficacy of a hedge fund's compliance policies and procedures is reviewed.

Testing Goals The primary goals of the compliance testing process are twofold: First, if during the testing process any actual policy violations are noted, then corrective action can be taken to resolve those issues. Second, the compliance testing process uses the information gathered during the testing process to determine if the hedge fund should take more general corrective action in certain areas. For example, if a number of violations in the specific area being tested are noted, employees may need additional training in that area. Alternatively, the testing process may show that policies and procedures in a particular area are too vague or too difficult to implement and should be revised to prevent violations going forward.

Specific Policy Testing To understand the way compliance testing works in practice, consider the example of a hedge fund's trade allocation policy, which is the way a hedge fund distributes or allocates completed trades among the various funds it manages. To test policy adherence in this area, the compliance function may review multiple completed trades to determine whether the firm's policy were indeed followed. This type of testing is sometimes referred to as *compliance back testing*, because of its backward-looking nature.

It is up to the compliance function to determine during what time period and how many trades should be reviewed. One factor that would influence these determinations is how frequently the compliance function has tested trade allocation policies in the past. A second factor is whether the hedge fund has had any previous compliance issues in this area. For example, if the hedge fund has had several violations of its trade allocation policy over a short period of time, then the compliance department may want to conduct more extensive and frequent testing in this area. Alternatively, the compliance function may wish to be less narrow in the selection of the specific time period during which to test and instead conduct a random review of trades over a broader period of time. This is commonly referred to as *random selection*.

Once the scope for the testing is determined, the actual testing can then occur. Continuing the trade allocation example, the compliance function would proceed with the testing by collecting the trading records to review during predetermined time periods. They would then compare the ways in which the trades were allocated among the hedge fund's different fund vehicles to determine whether any violations had occurred. If specific violations are noted, then corrective action would be taken to rectify the errors. In addition, such reviews may find instances in which it was close to a violation, although the full violation did not occur. This is referred to as a *near miss*, and many hedge fund compliance departments maintain a *near miss register*. By studying these near misses, the compliance department can make determinations about where potential weaknesses may exist in the compliance program and take corrective action accordingly before any true policy violations occur.

Firm-Wide Testing   The goal of firm-wide testing is to cast a broad net across a wide variety of compliance policies and procedures instead of focusing too heavily on a single particular issue or area. Typically, firm-wide testing is conducted on an ongoing basis according to a predetermined schedule known as a *compliance calendar*. This schedule may be organized in a number of different ways. For example, it may specify particular months for the testing of compliance policies in different departments of the firm, such as business development or trading. Alternatively, the compliance calendar could specify the testing of specific policies and procedures as opposed to departments, such as compliance procedures surrounding employee personal securities transactions.

Firm-wide testing is similar to the activities of a different department known as the *internal audit function*. Some larger hedge funds, or those affiliated with larger firms, may maintain in-house internal audit functions. This function typically picks a number of issues or departments throughout the firm and conducts testing on them on an ongoing basis. The difference between the two functions is that the internal audit function is not necessarily limited to compliance issues. The increasingly overlapping nature of the two functions has led many hedge funds that previously maintained dedicated internal audit personnel, to integrate many aspects of the internal audit function into the compliance function.

FIRM COMMITTEES AS COMPLIANCE MECHANISMS

So far we have focused on the common tasks performed by in-house hedge fund compliance departments and discussed how noncompliance professionals play ancillary roles in compliance as part of their daily jobs.

With this division between in-house compliance professionals and non-compliance professionals in mind, we can next turn to an area of hedge fund compliance known as *hedge fund committees*. These committees often serve to bridge the gap between the compliance duties of the in-house compliance professionals and noncompliance professionals.

Some common features of hedge fund committees include:

- *Not necessarily compliance focused*—Certain committees may be focused primarily on compliance-related matters while others may not. Examples of these other types of committees would be an investment committee and a compensation committee.
- *Committee membership*—In many instances, a committee will consist of both in-house compliance professionals and noncompliance professionals. Depending on the committee's role, there may be no compliance professionals on a committee; however, this does not mean the work of the committee is not subject to compliance oversight.
- *Committees provide oversight on a less frequent basis than employees*— Most committees do not meet daily but rather monthly, quarterly, or on an as-needed basis. To complement the oversight of committees, a hedge fund will typically have individuals in place that provide more frequent oversight of the specific issues that a committee will eventually address. Oftentimes, this more frequent oversight is rolled up to support the analysis of committees when they meet.
- *Committees do not operate in isolation*—Committees may have different focuses, but there is often overlap among them. For example, at a high level the work of a compliance committee is different from that of an information technology committee. However, if the information

technology committee is addressing a technology issue that will influence the implementation of the hedge fund's compliance policies, then the two committees would likely coordinate on this issue.

Regardless of whether a committee is focused exclusively on compliance-related matters, they often serve as a valuable control function and provide oversight regarding the firm-wide implementation of compliance policies and procedures.

Formal and Informal Committees

Hedge fund committees may be either formal or informal. *Informal committees* are traditionally more loosely structured as compared to *formal committees*. The characteristics of formal committees include:

- *Meeting frequency*—The committee meets with a predetermined frequency (i.e., quarterly).
- *Agenda and minutes*—A formal agenda is prepared (and perhaps distributed) prior to each meeting. At the meeting, the topics discussed and any decision made are formally documented *meeting minutes*. If a compliance professional is a committee member, they often serve as the meeting secretary and prepare the meeting minutes.
- *Defined list of members*—While other individuals may attend the committee meetings, a formal list of committee members is maintained. This formal membership is important because in certain instances committees are required to votes on certain issues. Typically, only formal members are allowed to cast votes; therefore, the makeup and number of committee members can be an important consideration.

Somewhat confusingly, an informal committee may also meet with a predetermined frequency, prepare an agenda and meeting minutes, and have regular members. If this is the case, then why does this distinction between informal and formal matter?

Informal committees are viewed as being less permanent. For example, a hedge fund could establish an informal committee to deal with a specific project, and once the project is complete the committee disbands. A historical example of this would be a hedge fund that created an informal committee to manage the process related to the first time it was planning to data-intensive regulatory filing, such as the U.S. Securities and Exchange Commission's Form PF. After the initial filing was completed, this committee may have then completed its tasks and been dissolved. Essentially, the committee had short-term goals. An example of a more formal, permanent committee would be a compliance committee as it will

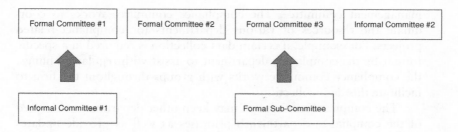

EXHIBIT 4.3 Example Hedge Fund Committee Structure

have compliance-related tasks and challenges that need to be overseen in perpetuity. It should also be noted that in some instances a formal committee may oversee the work of an informal committee.

Additionally, both formal and informal committees may have subcommittees, although it is less common in informal committees because they are generally already focused on specific-issues. Exhibit 4.3 shows an example of an oversight structure of formal and informal committees, as well as subcommittees.

Types of Committees

Generally, regulators will not mandate that a hedge fund maintain an extensive list of predetermined committees. As a result, committees vary in number and structure from firm to firm. A larger hedge fund that manages multiple strategies may find it useful to maintain a stand-alone committee focused on analyzing both fund-level and firm-wide exposure to different trading counterparties. Alternatively, a smaller hedge fund may find it more efficient to have counterparty risk analyzed by the firm's investment professionals with no specifically designated committee focused on the issue. Or the firm could include counterparty risk into the work of a different committee, perhaps one focused on all types of risk exposure.

What follows is a general description of common categories of hedge fund committees. Although the committees outlined below are typically organized as formal committees, they may also be seen as organized in an informal structure as well:

- *Compliance committee*—In addition to maintaining a distinct compliance function, a hedge fund may also maintain a formal compliance committee. Committee members usually include compliance professionals, such as the CCO, as well as individuals from other investment and operational departments. In addition, the compliance committee may be supported by other subcommittees, such as a conflict management committee. The compliance committee works to coordinate the resources of various departments for compliance-related projects. For example, if certain data collection is required in a specific format by the compliance department to assist with regulatory filings, the compliance committee works with groups throughout the firm to facilitate this data collection.

The compliance committee may keep other departments informed of the compliance department's priorities as well as provide updates on compliance trends. By disseminating this information through the compliance committee, the noncompliance focused committee members from other departments can share updates on compliance priorities with their respective departments. In this way, the compliance committee serves as another avenue to provide ongoing training and updates.

- *Management committee*—The management committee provides oversight on the overall management of the firm. This committee is often not directly involved in discussing specifics related to the firm's funds, but instead analyzes issues related to the continued growth of the firm and addresses operational challenges that arise. This committee sets the compliance tone of the hedge fund in collaboration with the compliance committee. Management committee members are typically a cross section of senior management of the firm's different departments, including a representative of the compliance function.

- *Investment committee*—Unlike the management committee, the investment committee is responsible for providing oversight of a hedge fund's investment activities. Investment committees often meet frequently (at least weekly). A hedge fund may have different investment committees for different investment strategies or a single committee that shares information across all strategies. A compliance representative may attend these meetings to provide guidance on the compliance impact of making certain investments or how to best ensure that compliance violations are avoided when structuring certain investments.

- *Risk committee*—A risk committee focuses on analyzing a hedge fund's risk exposures, including but not limited to funding and financial risks, counterparty risk, and operational risks. The committee may also analyze the regulatory risks posed by anticipated changes in financial regulations or new regulatory reporting requirements. A compliance professional is typically involved with the risk committee in assessing regulatory risks. As part of their oversight, risk committees may analyze different risk analyses, such as historical simulations and scenario analysis.

Depending on a number of factors, including the size of the hedge fund and its investment activities, multiple risk committees may be formed, each with a focus on a different risk area. These could be formal committees on their own or subcommittees of a larger over-arching risk committee. An example of this would be a stand-alone formal counterparty risk committee or an operational risk committee. The work of these individual risk committees could then either be analyzed individually or rolled up as part of a larger firm-wide risk review by the bigger risk committee.

- *Valuation committee*—Valuation presents a number of compliance challenges for hedge funds. Most keep documents that outline the way in which they value their investments. One such document is an ***offering memorandum*** (OM), and it contains a number of details and risk disclosures surrounding a potential investment. One section addresses the ways in which a hedge fund, along with its service providers, will value its securities. In practice, the language in OMs can be vague and not reflect the actual valuation practices employed by the hedge fund. To bridge this gap, a separate ***valuation policy*** is typically maintained. Valuation policies generally contain more detail of the valuation process used in practice, such as the actual valuation sources utilized for specific securities.

  The role of the valuation committee is to ensure compliance with the firm's valuation policies and procedures. As a result, the role of the committee is heavily rooted in compliance-related matters, including ensuring that internal valuation memoranda are produced to support valuation changes. In addition, if the hedge fund has any strategies that invest in positions that are priced by the hedge fund, rather than by third parties, then the valuation committee would play a role in overseeing the documentation to support this pricing.

  Due to the importance of developing and maintaining this documentation as well as the large degree of interaction with the compliance department in overseeing this documentation, the CCO is typically a voting member of the valuation committee.

There are other committees that may be formed to oversee a broad range of areas of a fund's operations, including a business continuity and disaster recovery committee, a technology steering committee, a best execution committee, and a strategic planning committee.

CHAPTER SUMMARY

This chapter began by providing a refresher on the distinctions between dedicated, shared, and noncompliance personnel. We next addressed the common tasks performed by compliance functions under the guidance of the CCO. This included an overview of compliance training and testing duties. Including firm-wide and issue-specific training were discussed. Specific policy-level and firm-wide testing approaches were then discussed. Finally, the role of hedge fund committees, both formal and informal, as compliance mechanisms was discussed.

At the end of these first four chapters, we have developed an initial understanding of the ways in which departments outside of the compliance function itself play a role in bolstering the overall compliance efforts of the hedge fund. In the next chapter, we will look at the ways hedge fund technology increasingly expands both the effectiveness and challenges of the compliance department.

NOTE

1. See J. William, "Managers Face Swiss Legal Representative Requirement," *HedgeWeek*, February 24, 2015.

CHAPTER 5

Hedge Fund Compliance Technology

INTRODUCTION

Hedge funds, like the vast majority of businesses in the modern world, are heavy users of technology. The bulk of hedge funds utilize technology to assist in the management and execution of their investment strategies. Information technology (IT) is also a critical element to the noninvestment aspects of hedge fund operations. The range of technology utilized can vary from more generalized technologies, such as e-mail or electronic collaboration systems such as Microsoft SharePoint, to more hedge fund–specific technologies, such as specialized fund accounting systems.

UNDERSTANDING THE HEDGE FUND INFORMATION TECHNOLOGY FUNCTION

Similar to the ways in which hedge funds typically maintain functions that perform compliance-related duties, so too do hedge funds have IT functions. In order to understand how compliance is involved working with the IT function we must first understand how hedge fund IT functions are organized. At a high level, hedge funds, like most modern businesses, maintain three broad categories of IT focus: a hardware function, a software function, and a help desk function.

1. *Hardware function*—The hardware function refers to the section of the IT function that focuses on supporting the physical equipment required to maintain a hedge fund's IT function. This can include items such as servers, routers, cables, and generators. In many instances, the hardware

side of the IT function is also responsible for hardware related to other more daily tasks such as printers and telephones.

2. *Software function*—The software function refers to the work of the IT group that supports the nonhardware aspects of a hedge fund's technology needs. This includes supporting standard office software, such as word processing and e-mail, as well as more technical software, such as for the management of production servers, data backup, and storage applications, database management applications, as well as software to manage Internet access. Depending on their needs, hedge funds may also seek to develop or customize their own software. When a hedge fund develops software, this is also typically classified under the software function of the IT group.

3. *Help desk function*—Depending on the structure of the hedge fund's IT group, a hedge fund may also maintain a dedicated *help desk function*. This function, commonly referred to as help desks, provides ongoing support to a hedge fund's employees if an issue arises that typically leads to a disruption in the continued functionality of hardware or software critical to employees' jobs. The help desk will then proceed to diagnose and attempt to fix the problem. In some cases, the same IT department employees that perform hardware and software functions also serve as help desk support. In other instances, there are dedicated help desk employees, or the help desk is outsourced to a third-party service provider.

Information Technology Function Structure

There are many similarities between the ways in which IT and compliance functions may be organized. One way that IT functions are similar to compliance functions is that IT functions will typically consist of in-house personnel who are employees of the hedge fund. Similar to compliance these employees may be either dedicated or shared in their IT focus, depending on the resources and needs of the hedge fund. In addition, third-party IT consultants may also augment the IT work of any internal hedge fund personnel. In certain instances, the IT function may be completely outsourced to third-party IT consultants.

The individual who leads the IT function is referred to as the **Chief Technology Officer** (CTO). Exhibit 5.1 provides an example of a representative structure of a hedge fund's IT function. Please note that, in the exhibit the software, hardware, and help desk support functions are also labeled based on the grouping of the individuals by title and reporting structure, respectively.

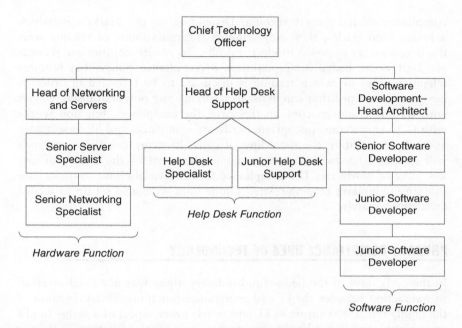

EXHIBIT 5.1 Representative Structure of a Hedge Fund Information Technology Function

Compliance Considerations For Different IT Functions

Depending on the nature of the specific IT function, different compliance considerations are in place. For example, consider the software function within a hedge fund. If the hedge fund is engaged in developing its own proprietary software, then the compliance function should develop and maintain policies regarding the electronic storage and access of this software. Hedge fund compliance personnel, however, may not be familiar with all of the technical ins-and-outs regarding storing and securing proprietary software. In these instances, it is up to the compliance personnel to collaborate with a hedge fund's in-house IT professionals, or its consultants, to develop an understanding of best practices in this area. Furthermore, once these policies are in place the compliance department must also work with IT to develop appropriate policies to ensure adequate testing of adherence to the original policies in place.

With regards to the hardware IT function, an example of the ways compliance may be involved is in regard to working with IT to ensure that a hedge fund's hardware is set up appropriately to facilitate required compliance-related record keeping. Depending on the markets in which a hedge fund trades, they may conduct a large volume of trading over the telephone as opposed to electronically. To ensure appropriate records are kept, some hedge funds maintain a compliance policy that requires telephone lines on which trading is discussed to be recorded in order to have a voice record that can assist in resolving any potential discrepancies with trading counterparties. In this case, the compliance function works with IT to ensure the appropriate hardware is in place, and likely software as well, to facilitate the recording of calls. In many cases, hedge funds will maintain hardware redundancies in the event of the failure of any key piece of hardware. The compliance function would have to make sure that any redundant trading-related phone lines were also set up to record calls appropriately.

PRIMARY COMPLIANCE USES OF TECHNOLOGY

In the early days of the hedge fund industry, there was not much overlap or interaction between the IT and compliance functions. Today, because of the highly integrated nature of IT into nearly every aspect of a hedge fund's operations, compliance has become increasingly involved in both:

1. Utilizing technology to carry out the specific work of the compliance function; and
2. Leveraging IT to ensure that the implementation and oversight of fund and employee-level activities are consistent with a hedge fund's compliance policies and procedures.

A third area that has become increasingly important with regard to the interaction between compliance and IT relates to the issue of *technology risk* to hedge funds. Technology risk can be defined as the business risk associated with the use, ownership, operation, involvement, influence, and adoption of IT within an enterprise.[1]

Another concept that has become increasingly important from a compliance perspective is *cybersecurity*. From the perspective of hedge fund regulators, there is no universally recognized definition of cybersecurity. In practice, it is a broad term that can encompass a wide variety of considerations and risks, depending on the context. For the purposes of our discussion, we will define cybersecurity as the risks associated with maintaining the integrity of a hedge funds IT security and architecture, with a focus on protecting data and intellectual property from unauthorized access or theft. The risks associated with cybersecurity can include penetration into a hedge fund's computer systems by unauthorized third parties, such as hackers, and the risks of the theft of data by the firm's own employees. Cybersecurity within hedge funds is discussed in more detail in Chapter 11.

COMPLIANCE CONSIDERATIONS FOR USE OF ELECTRONIC DATA

One of the major hedge fund compliance technology considerations is in electronically stored information. This information comes about in two primary forms: electronic communication and electronic data.

Hedge funds communicate with various groups, including service providers and clients, through electronic means. In addition, hedge funds generate electronic communications information through in-house communication among a firm's own employees. This electronic communication is not just through e-mail but via other avenues, including instant messaging, and communication through other popular trading and research systems, such has Bloomberg. Electronic data, on the other hand, refers to the wide variety of other types of electronic information hedge funds create, including spreadsheets, research memos, and marketing presentations.

Financial regulators generally require that hedge funds archive both types of electronic information. In addition, regulators often typically require that hedge funds monitor electronic communications by their employees. Due to the electronic nature of this communication, these processes are typically conducted utilizing various software programs in conjunction with human oversight.

Increased Use of Electronic Data by Hedge Funds

Historically, the majority of information at a hedge fund was kept in a hard-copy paper format. For example, a fund may have kept a physical record of proposed trades in a paper trade blotter. Another trading-related example would be if a hedge fund maintained actual physical trade tickets filled out by its traders that may have been time-stamped to show the time the trade was executed. Today, the use of hard-copy paper records has largely been phased out as technology has continued to evolve, primarily because it is easy to create redundant archives of electronic data. Electronic data are also easier to share and access as compared with paper copy data.

Compliance Benefits of Utilizing Electronic Data

As regulators have increased their focus on record-keeping requirements for hedge funds, compliance departments have sought to embrace the use of electronic records over paper records. A main benefit from a compliance perspective is the ability to search electronic data much more easily as compared with hard copy data. This ability to search data is particularly helpful for monitoring electronic data and in responding to specific regulatory requests.

A second benefit is the ability to better restrict access to data. This is particularly important from a compliance perspective where a hedge fund's policies often require the protection of hedge fund's proprietary data, such as the computer code for an internally developed trading algorithm or a database of investor contact information. Not every employee needs access to every piece of data to perform their daily jobs, and the compliance function can work with the IT function to implement policies to limit access as required.

A third benefit of utilizing electronic as opposed to paper data is that compliance can better track who accesses stored data. Assume that someone who is unauthorized to access a specific trading algorithm does so. A record is generated of this unauthorized access and the employee can be questioned about why they took this action. Developing and maintaining these types of records is important from a compliance perspective in part to facilitate any regulatory inquiries regarding such incidents.

A fourth benefit of electronic data is that not only can a hedge fund restrict and track access to certain data but also can better control the method by which it is accessed. Assume there is an employee who works as a programmer. Further assume that she is authorized to access a specific trading algorithm on her desktop terminal located in the office and does so. Let us further assume that she then wants to work from home and later that day attempts to access the file remotely from her personal computer at home over the secure work network. A hedge fund may not want the programmer to do this in order to protect the integrity of its proprietary information. The compliance department could work with IT to develop policies to limit access to this confidential data only from inside the office.

A fifth benefit of using electronic data relates to the ability to implement enhanced security surrounding electronic data. Assume that the programmer in the previous example instead attempted to download the trading algorithm directly from the computer in her office to what is known as a *remote storage device* (a physical piece of portable hardware on which data can be stored), such as CD-ROM disks, USB drives, or external hard drives. To prevent employees from taking data outside the office, a hedge fund may implement restrictions on downloading data to these remote storage devices. In addition, even if data may be downloaded onto a remote storage device, the fact that these data are stored in an electronic format also allows a hedge fund to implement a number of additional security measures, such as password protections on files.

A final compliance benefit of the use of electronic data as opposed to paper data relates to the ability to label and customize client-facing documentation. Hedge funds are generally under regulatory obligations to track which data are sent to prospective and existing clients. In the past, this was historically done through numbering or labeling systems. For example, when distributing a marketing presentation, commonly referred to as a *pitchbook*, to a prospective investor it would not be uncommon for the compliance department to sequentially number the presentations being sent out and to keep a record of which number presentation was sent to which prospective client. To further enhance protections in this regard, many hedge funds now utilize technology that allows for the automatic labeling and record keeping of what material is sent to different clients. In addition, many of these technologies also insert automatic watermarks on documentation. These watermarks can be used to label each page of the documentation with a specific piece of information, such as an e-mail address, related to the client to whom the electronic document was distributed.

Electronic Communication Policies and Procedures A key compliance consideration for hedge funds electronic data is the development of policies regarding the use, monitoring, and archiving of electronic data. As outlined below, there are several key questions that a hedge fund's compliance function should consider when designing these policies:

What types of data need to be archived?

One of the first items hedge funds must consider is what types of electronic data need to be archived. It would be easy to say that a hedge fund should just archive everything, but this is not always practical or desired, and not every hedge fund has the resources to do this.

From a regulatory perspective, in the United States, SEC Rule 204-2 of the Investment Advisers Act of 1940 (Advisers Act), the so-called *Books and Records Rule*, provides guidance in this regard. According to guidance from the U.S. Securities and Exchange Commission's staff of the Investment Management and Office of Compliance Inspections and Examinations, examples of the types of records that this rule requires Investment Advisers, including registered hedge funds, to retain include:[2]

- *Financial and accounting records*—This includes cash receipts and disbursements journals, income and expense account ledgers, checkbooks, bank account statements, business bills, and financial statements.
- *Investment records*—Hedge funds covered by this SEC Rule are required to retain records relating to providing investment advice and

transactions in client accounts, including trade orders, trade confirmation statements from broker-dealers, documentation of proxy vote decisions, withdrawal requests and documentation of client deposits received, and correspondence with existing or potential clients.

■ *Designation of discretionary authority by clients*—This includes documentation that details a hedge fund's authority to conduct business in client accounts, including a list of accounts in which a manager has discretionary authority, the documentation that grants the manager discretionary authority, and written agreements with clients.

■ *Existing and prospective client communications*—Examples of these types of documents are any hedge fund advertising and performance records, including any client newsletters, articles, and worksheets demonstrating performance returns.

■ *Code of ethics documentation*—Hedge funds covered by the Rule are required to maintain records relating to a hedge fund's **Code of Ethics**. In the United States, under SEC Rule 204A-1, the so-called Code of Ethics Rule of the Advisers Act, hedge funds are required to maintain a document commonly known as the Code of Ethics, which is a policy document outlining permissible business conduct of personnel, including those addressing personal securities transaction reporting (and is discussed in more detail in Chapter 7).

■ *Disclosure documentation*—Covered hedge funds are required to maintain records relating to the maintenance and delivery to prospective and existing clients of what are known as **disclosure documentation** and **supplements** under SEC Rule 204-3. These documents are sometimes referred to as disclosure brochures and typically refers to regulatory filings such as Form ADV.

■ *Annual compliance review documentation*—SEC Rule 206(4)-7, known as the Compliance Rule, outlines that registered hedge funds are required to maintain compliance programs. As part of these programs, hedge funds are required to prepare an annual review of their compliance programs. The guidance in this case outlines that covered hedge funds should maintain documentation of the policies and procedures adopted and implemented under the Compliance Rule, including any documentation prepared in the course of their annual required compliance reviews.

Do you have a written policy for data retention?

Hedge fund compliance departments may fall into the trap of assuming that the IT function is automatically backing up all data, all the time. This is not always the case, and it may not be practical to do so. In addition, employees outside of the IT function may be unclear as to what data they may need to proactively archive. Written policies created by the compliance department, coupled with appropriate enforcement of these policies, can work to alleviate these problems.

Data retention policies may be stand-alone policies or contained within other compliance documents, such as a compliance manual. In addition to addressing any specific requirements mandated by regulators, there are a number of practical considerations hedge funds should address in developing these policies. An example of such a stand-alone policy that would reference electronic communication protocols, in addition to other cybersecurity policies, would be a Written Information Security Plan (WISP), discussed in Chapter 11.

Where should data be archived?

Using the SEC Rule 204-2 guidance, the SEC staff outlines that records are required to be kept in an easily accessible location. With increased acknowledgment of the importance of business continuity and disaster recovery planning, hedge funds are increasingly storing data in multiple locations to protect against a disaster event, which could destroy data in any single location. With regards to electronic data, increasingly hedge funds are storing data in the *cloud*. As cloud technology has evolved, compliance departments should work with the IT function to properly understand the cloud environment in place, including what types of clouds are being utilized (public versus private) and the security protocols in place to protect data stored on the cloud.

How frequently should data be backed up?

Another compliance consideration in developing policies in this area relates to how frequently data should be backed up as part of the archiving process. In practice, hedge funds may perform less frequent backups of what they may consider to be less critical data and more frequent backups of other data. The frequency of data backups is an area in which the compliance function may benefit from technology guidance from the IT group in regards to the practical limitations of archiving a considerable amount of data.

How long must data be archived for?

In addition to regulatory guidance regarding what data must be archived, there are also guidelines with regard to the amount of time it must be kept. In the United States, for example, Rule 204-2 states that data must generally be kept by hedge funds for at least five years and, in some cases, up to seven years. In practice, depending on the volume of the data and the resources of the hedge funds, a hedge fund may decide to take a conservative approach and to archive all data in perpetuity; however, this requires more resources to do so and may not be practical in all cases.

COMPLIANCE OVERSIGHT OF NONELECTRONIC DATA

Although hedge funds store the majority of information electronically, for reasons that include legacy practices and resource constraints, they may still store certain data in nonelectronic formats. An example of the type of hard-copy documents that may be stored would be brokerage statements collected by the compliance function in relation to the oversight of trading in their own personal accounts. Another common example would be hard copy forms used to collect the physical signatures of employees with authority to approve cash transfers for the payment of vendor invoices by the hedge fund.

In some cases, the compliance group may work with the IT group to create electronic solutions to phase out the use of these hard-copy forms. This can be done through the implementation of new software systems to replace old hard-copy approval processes and the scanning of legacy physical forms into electronic data input formats.

BUSINESS CONTINUITY AND DISASTER RECOVERY PLANNING

Business continuity and disaster recovery planning (BCP/DR) is an area of increased importance for hedge funds and represents another key area in which the compliance and IT functions overlap. Business disruptions can occur for a wide variety of reasons. These range from the more commonplace disruption in utilities, such as phone service, Internet connectivity, or power outages to more widespread disaster events, such as terrorism or extreme weather, including Hurricane Sandy, which disrupted the operations of many hedge funds in the northeast United States in 2012.

While it is a good business practice to ensure that a hedge fund can continue operations in the event of disruption, increasingly regulators are also mandating that hedge funds develop written *business continuity and disaster recovery policy documents* that outline a hedge fund's plans to deal with BCP/DR events. As an example, in the United States, the National Futures Association Compliance Rule 2-38 requires hedge funds registered with the NFA to adopt business continuity and disaster recovery plans.[3]

Another example is the guidance provided by the SEC with regard to Rule 206(4)-7, which outlines in part, "*We believe that an adviser's fiduciary obligation to its clients includes the obligation to take steps to protect the clients' interests from being placed at risk as a result of the adviser's inability to provide advisory services after, for example, a natural disaster or, in the case of some smaller firms, the death of the owner or key personnel.*

The clients of an adviser that is engaged in the active management of their assets would ordinarily be placed at risk if the adviser ceased operations."[4]
Key areas typically addressed in a BCP/DR plan include:

- Data backup and recovery.
- Developing communication plans so key employees can communicate in the event of a disaster event, including the use of tools such as a *calling tree*.
- Clarification regarding the process by which employees can continue to work while outside the office. This can include details of remote employee secure access and the ability to continue trading via alternative measures, such as through the use of mobile phones.
- Designating alternative locations from which employees may continue operations. This includes designating a formal location, known as a *disruption gathering location*, where employees would be directed to go in the event of disruptions, which render a hedge fund's office inaccessible.
- Details of how communications with investors and fund service providers should continue in the event of a business disruption.

Another key component of BCP/DR planning compliance departments now focus on is continued testing of said plans once implemented. While plan testing may be coordinated by departments other than compliance, such as a hedge fund's IT department, the compliance department is often instrumental in ensuring that plans are tested according to a predetermined schedule and that testing is documented appropriately.

CHAPTER SUMMARY

We focused on the interaction between hedge fund compliance and technology. We began by discussing the three primary areas of hedge fund IT functions: hardware, software, and a help desk function. Next, we discussed the primary ways in which the compliance function utilizes technology. We then addressed the considerable role of compliance in developing policies for the monitoring and archiving of electronic communication and data. This discussion included an overview of the numerous compliance benefits to hedge funds that embrace the use of electronic as opposed to hard copy data. Finally, we addressed the role played by compliance in developing business continuity and disaster recovery policies.

The compliance function is increasingly tasked with addressing the challenges and opportunities presented by the increased use of technology. In the next chapter, we will discuss ways in hedge funds work with service providers , including compliance consultants to augment their compliance functions and assist in meeting these emerging challenges.

NOTES

1. ISACA, "The Risk IT Framework," 2009.
2. U.S. SEC, "Information for Newly-Registered Investment Advisers," www.sec .gov/divisions/investment/advoverview.htm#P6_208.
3. National Futures Association, "Interpretive Notice 9052—NFA Compliance Rule 2-38: Business Continuity and Disaster Recovery Plan," July 1, 2003.
4. U.S. SEC, "Final Rule: Compliance Programs of Investment Companies and Investment Advisers," www.sec.gov/rules/final/ia-2204.htm#P102_22999.

CHAPTER **6**

Compliance Consultants and Other Compliance-Related Service Providers

SERVICE PROVIDER COMPLIANCE

Until this point in our reading, we have centered our discussion on a hedge fund's in-house compliance resources. In addition to in-house compliance personnel, hedge funds may also utilize third-party firms known as service providers to assist in the performance of their compliance requirements. Service providers are individuals or firms that are not employees of the hedge fund but provide services to it.

CLASSIFICATION OF COMPLIANCE SERVICE PROVIDERS

Hedge fund service providers may offer a wide variety of compliance-related services to hedge funds. Historically, from a compliance perspective, service providers were grouped into two primary categories within compliance-related services. The first group provided primarily compliance-focused services to hedge funds. One such service provider would have been a *compliance consultant. A compliance consultant is a* third-party firm, or individual, that advises on compliance-related matters. The second group provided primarily non-compliance-focused services, such as a fund administrator, a bank, or a hedge fund's auditor.

In recent years, however, hedge fund service providers, whether compliance focused or not, have broadened their service offerings. Service providers that historically would not have offered compliance-related services now offer them. Therefore, a more appropriate modern approach toward analyzing the role of hedge fund service providers is to focus on the actual compliance-related services performed rather than on which type of firm offers these services.

This distinction is important for two primary reasons. First, it is important to the hedge fund when analyzing the resources, both in-house and external, available to the compliance function. For example, if multiple service providers utilized by a hedge fund offer overlapping compliance services, then it may make sense to consolidate these services under one provider for reasons relating to efficiency or cost savings. In addition, just because a service provider offers a compliance-related service, the hedge fund may not want to have a third party perform this service at all, and may elect to bring it in-house.

The second reason this distinction is important is from the perspective of a hedge fund's potential investors seeking to evaluate the compliance function. Using the traditional classification approach, if an investor sought only to evaluate a hedge fund's so-called compliance consultants, then they may overlook other traditional noncompliance service providers that now offer compliance-related services. The investor evaluation of compliance function is discussed in more detail in Chapter 8.

SERVICE PROVIDER COMPLIANCE WORK

Different hedge fund service providers assist with hedge fund compliance-related work in a number of ways. To understand how such services are performed, let's examine the role of a service provider known as a fund administrator. A *fund administrator* commonly performs duties related to portfolio valuation and reporting. With regard to the valuation work, one of the key components that outlines the way in which securities will be contained are in sections of a document known as the *offering memorandum* (OM). OMs are specific to each of the different managed funds and detail a wide variety of fund terms and disclaimers surrounding a potential investment. The fund administrator utilizes the valuation guidance contained in the OM to assist the hedge fund in complying its technical valuation requirements. While complying with the terms of an OM is different from complying with specific regulatory guidance, such as an SEC rule, both types of compliance are still important for hedge funds, and indeed regulators do focus on whether hedge funds have complied with their offering documentation as well.

Another example of the way in which service providers assist with compliance-related work would be by examining the role of the fund *auditor*. An auditor, among other tasks, prepares a hedge fund's audited financial statements. For U.S.-domiciled hedge fund vehicles, audited financial statements are traditionally prepared under an accounting standard known as U.S. Generally Accepted Accounting Principles (U.S. GAAP). It is the auditor's responsibility to ensure the financial statements comply with U.S. GAAP.

In other cases, service providers may focus directly on more traditional regulatory compliance-related work, such as a hedge fund's legal counsel. Historically, in addition to pure legal work, law firms were heavily involved in the compliance process and performed a wide variety of regulatory compliance-related tasks, ranging from assisting hedge funds in completing their initial registration with regulators to ongoing compliance monitoring and training. Today, hedge funds still work with law firms for compliance-related matters; however, in the majority of instances a large volume of compliance work has largely transitioned to compliance consultants.

HEDGE FUND COMPLIANCE CONSULTANTS

Traditionally, hedge funds consulted with external legal counsel to assist in regulatory compliance matters. Over time, the increasingly complex nature of compliance work created a need in the marketplace for specialized compliance consultants.

To be clear, there are no regulatory requirements that insist a hedge fund must utilize the services of a compliance consultant as opposed to a law firm for compliance-related matters. In fact, a hedge fund is not required to utilize a compliance consultant at all if they do not want to and may instead handle all compliance matters in-house or through a different service provider such as a law firm.

Reasons for the Increased Use of Compliance Consultants

There has been a trend in recent years for hedge funds to increasingly utilize compliance consultants for their specialized knowledge and expertise, including:

- *Increased complexity of hedge fund compliance*—The increased complexity of compliance guidelines globally has resulted in hedge funds developing a need for specialized knowledge and familiarity in interpreting these compliance rules. Compliance consultants have increasingly stepped in to fill this niche.
- *Supporting internal compliance resources*—The overall volume of compliance-related work has increased in recent years. This includes enhanced requirements for regulatory reporting and ongoing monitoring of the implementation of compliance policies and procedures

within hedge funds. As a result, compliance consultants are utilized increasingly by hedge funds to assist with their growing needs in this area.

- *Demand for former regulatory experience*—Many compliance consultants employ personnel who have formerly worked at financial regulators. This direct familiarity with regulatory processes can assist hedge funds in navigating the regulatory compliance process and in dealing with regulators.
- *Cost-effectiveness*—Not every hedge fund has the resources or desire to develop its own internal compliance function to adequately address all of its compliance needs. This may be particularly true in newly launched or smaller hedge funds. In these cases, a compliance consultant can provide a cost-effective solution for funds.

Services Offered by Compliance Consultants

Hedge fund compliance consultants may perform a wide variety of services including:

- Registering a hedge fund with regulators
- Drafting compliance policies and procedures
- Regulatory reporting support
- Testing and monitoring of compliance procedures
- Assisting with internal audit or investigations
- Performing mock regulatory audits
- Education and training on compliance-related matters
- Facilitating regular compliance review such as annual compliance reviews

Depending on the nature of the services, compliance consultants may bill hedge funds at prespecified contract rates or at hourly rates.

Outsourced Chief Compliance Officers

Some compliance consultants serve as an outsourced *Chief Compliance Officer* (CCO). In these cases, the compliance consultant would designate a specific individual from their consultancy to serve as the designee CCO. This would be as opposed to naming an actual employee of the hedge fund as CCO. Whether a hedge fund should outsource the CCO function to a compliance consultant is increasingly debated in the hedge fund community.

Arguments against Outsourcing the CCO Function   Common arguments raised against outsourcing the CCO function to a compliance consultant include:

- *Lack of process ownership*—Some feel this may create a lack of owner-ship of the compliance function by the hedge fund since a third party is leading the function.
- *Potential for lower quality of compliance oversight*—An in-house CCO, even if they are shared and work on other functions, is typically engaged on a day-to-day basis with the compliance elements of a hedge fund. In outsourced CCO situations, the CCO is typically not on-site at the offices of the hedge fund every day. The thinking goes that because of the importance of integrating compliance into daily procedures, a dedicated in-house individual provides a higher level of compliance over-sight. Highlighting this point, some hedge funds have the CCO sit on or near the trading desk to further imbue this constant compliance over-sight. With an outsourced CCO, such a daily presence on areas such as trading desks is often lacking.
- *Potential for information barriers*—While certainly not advisable, an outsourced CCO may be limited in the information she receives from a fund manager because the fund proactively seeks to limit the involve-ment of an outside individual, even though that person serves as the CCO. The reason for this may be that a hedge fund incorrectly takes the position that the outsourced CCO is there to ensure minimum regula-tory compliance and that the hedge fund, not the service provider, knows what is the best interest in all areas of the firm's operations including compliance. In addition, perhaps the outsourced CCO does not wish to lean on the hedge fund too hard by requesting what the hedge fund may deem to be too much information for fear that the hedge fund might simply terminate them and replace them with a more amenable out-sourced CCO. As a result, information barriers may exist, and limit the effectiveness of the outsourced CCO.
- *Reduced frequency of ongoing monitoring*—With the exception of specific regulatory requirements to analyze a compliance program, such as the SEC requirement to conduct annual compliance reviews, hedge funds may decide to not engage outsourced CCOs to conduct any more frequent reviews. While technically meeting formal requirements, a hedge fund benefits from more frequent oversight and analysis of its compliance programs. The thinking goes that an in-house CCO resource would be better able to perform this ongoing monitoring.

Arguments in Favor of Outsourcing the CCO Function In a perfect world, every hedge fund would have a well-resourced in-house compliance function. This compliance function would include a mix of compliance generalists as well as specialists to address any of the specific compliance needs a hedge fund would require. In the real world, many hedge funds face practical resource constraint issues that limit the capital and resources they can devote to the compliance function. In addition, as compliance has become increasingly complex, the amount of time and resources hedge funds are required to devote, often referred to as the *cost of compliance*, has steadily increased. In these cases, as hedge funds become more resource and capital constrained they may benefit from transitioning from a dedicated CCO model to either a shared or outsourced model.

Some of the common advantages cited for utilizing an outsourced CCO include:

- *Increased specialization*—An in-house CCO may be limited in their knowledge of evolving regulatory compliance practices. Oftentimes, outsourced CCOs are part of a larger compliance consulting firm and can leverage the firm's expertise for knowledge on new compliance regulations. In addition, as hedge funds enter into new markets, specialized knowledge may be required to ensure ongoing compliance with different regulatory requirements.
- *Multiple fund coverage affords knowledge of industry trends*—Outsourced CCOs typically serve in this role for multiple hedge funds at the same time. One benefit of this is that they are able to develop an understanding of best practices in place across their many different hedge fund clients. As a result, the outsourced CCO's hedge fund clients will benefit from this experience in developing and providing ongoing oversight of their compliance function.
- *Increased efficiency and cost savings*—On a pure cost basis, it is often much more cost effective for a hedge fund to hire an outsourced CCO as opposed to staffing this function in-house.

Outsourced CCO Best Practices

As the outsourced CCO model continues to receive interest from hedge funds, regulators have increasingly scrutinized this practice. A study conducted by the SEC in November 2015 attempted to evaluate funds' compliance programs and the outsourced CCO role in the following areas:[1]

- *Compliance program design*—Was the compliance program reasonably designed to prevent, detect, and address violations?

- *Service provider communication*—Did the compliance program support open communication between service providers and those with compliance oversight responsibilities?
- *Proactive compliance*—Did the compliance program appear to be proactive rather than reactive?
- *CCO resources*—Did the CCO allocate sufficient resources to perform his or her responsibilities?
- *Culture of compliance*—Did compliance appear to be an important part of the fund's culture?
- *Authority and influence*—Did the CCO appear to have sufficient authority to influence adherence to compliance policies and procedures?

The best practices among registered funds included in the study that did outsource the CCO function were noted in three primary areas:

1. *Communication*—Not surprisingly, the SEC found that outsourced CCOs that frequently and personally interacted with fund employees maintained a better understanding of the fund's businesses, operations, and risks. This was compared to the practice of an outsourced CCO communicating with funds primarily through email and conducting their duties via predefined checklists.
2. *Resources*—The SEC noted that outsourced CCOs should not be stretched too thin by serving as an outsourced CCO for too many different funds and instead focus on a smaller number of funds.
3. *Empowerment*—In conducting annual compliance reviews, the outsourced CCO should have the ability to independently obtain records as opposed to relying exclusively on the fund's employees to provide them.

Some of the key deficiencies noted by the SEC study among funds that utilized outsourced CCOs were in the following areas:

- *Missing compliance policies*—Several funds did not have the policies, procedures, or disclosures in place necessary to address all the conflicts of interest identified in critical areas, including compensation practices, portfolio valuation, brokerage and execution, and personal securities transactions.
- *Not adhering to compliance policies*—Instances were noted in which the fund's compliance policies and procedures differed from the actual policies in place. In many instances, the outsourced CCOs were responsible for conducting reviews to test this adherence and, therefore, were derelict in this duty.

- *Overuse of compliance templates*—Several of the compliance manuals of funds were created utilizing prewritten outsourced CCO templates, which were not tailored to the specific practices in place at the funds under review. Examples of some of the compliance issues noted as a result of this included:
  - *Compliance policy omission*—Critical areas were not identified in compliance manuals; therefore, the appropriate procedures were not adopted relating to areas that included safeguarding client information.
  - *Adoption of incorrect policies*—Policies were adopted that were not applicable to fund businesses. This included collecting management fees quarterly in advance when in practice clients were billed monthly in arrears and referencing departed employees as responsible for performing compliance reviews and monitoring.
  - *Weak compliance controls*—Critical control procedures were not performed at all or not performed as described. Examples of areas in which deficiencies were noted included in the oversight of fee and expense allocations, reviews of solicitation activities for compliance, trade allocation reviews for fairness of side-by-side management of client accounts with proprietary accounts, oversight of performance advertising and marketing, personal trading reviews of all access persons, and controls over trade reconciliations.

Studies, such as this, outline that if a hedge fund opts to utilize an outsourced CCO they must be actively involved and engaged with the fund in order to fulfill not just the technical aspects of the CCO role, but also to impart a culture of compliance throughout the hedge fund.

Common Tasks Performed by Outsourced CCOs

When a hedge fund utilizes an outsourced CCO, two of the common tasks they perform are electronic communication monitoring and oversight of trading by the hedge fund employees for their own personal accounts. While an outsourced CCO could perform these tasks, in their absence the functions may be performed by in-house compliance personnel as well.

Electronic Communication Monitoring In Chapter 5, we discussed how hedge fund employees communicate electronically both internally and with external parties, such as trading counterparties and clients. The methods of these communications included e-mail, instant messaging, and trading and research systems such has Bloomberg and Reuters.

The compliance function is traditionally tasked with performing ongoing monitoring of these electronic communications to detect any potential compliance violations. Ideally, all electronic communications are monitored on an ongoing basis by compliance; however, this is not always practical. Hedge funds employ a variety of approaches to monitor samples of electronic communications. The thinking is that reviewing a sample of these communications may assist in determining whether any violations occurred. The methods of monitoring these communications depend on both the technical sophistication of the hedge funds communications as well as the resources employed in this area.

At its most basic level, a hedge fund may utilize a common e-mail platform such as Microsoft Outlook. Compliance personnel can perform a fairly straightforward search and simply go into a log of Outlook e-mails to search e-mails. Another approach is for the hedge fund to utilize specialized electronic communication monitoring software.

Once the technical ability to search electronic communications is in place, the next question becomes through what method and how frequently are communications monitored. One common method is a *keyword approach*, sometimes referred to as a *lexicon-based approach*. Under this methodology, a compliance professional searches electronic communications utilizing a predetermined list of words. These are typically words associated with potential compliance violations such as "guarantee" or "gift." A common problem with lexicon-based approaches is that a number of so-called false positive hits arise when performing these searches. That is, electronic communications are flagged when the word *gift* is used, but they do not relate to a compliance violation of the firm's gifts and entertainment policy but simply a normal use of the word *gift*. This particularly happens around the holidays when employees may be exchanging e-mails discussing gifts that may be permitted by the firm's compliance policies.

To rectify the issue, compliance professionals may also utilize an approach that focuses on selecting a random percentage of electronic communications to review. There are no bright-line rules about what constitutes the appropriate percentage of e-mails to review, and it is largely dependent on the firm's compliance resources in this area. In addition, distinctions may be drawn regarding whether compliance should review a random sampling of electronic communications across the entire firm or, instead, whether a certain percentage of each department's e-mails is reviewed. Another consideration is the frequency with which these reviews are conducted.

To illustrate how this works in practice, as an example, the compliance function may determine that it is going to review at least 5 percent of all firm-wide electronic communications on a monthly basis. Alternatively, the compliance function could decide to alternate among different departments on a rolling basis and opt to review 10 percent of all of the hedge fund's client service department's emails during one quarter and then review 10 percent of the investment team's e-mails the following quarter. These rules are not set in stone. If the compliance function grows concerned that a particular area of the firm becomes more exposed to potential compliance violations, such as the client service function in communication with prospective clients, then they could of course review a higher percentage of communications in this area as opposed to others.

Mock Regulatory Audits   Another service commonly offered by compliance consultants is a *mock audit,* sometimes referred to as a *mock regulatory audit*. This is a compliance review meant to simulate the examinations a regulator would conduct of a hedge fund. Typically, mock audits simulate *routine regulatory examinations*. Routine examinations were discussed in detail in Chapter 2.

Arguments in favor and against having compliance consultants perform mock regulatory audits
The primary advantage of having a compliance consultant perform a mock audit is that after completing such a review a hedge fund is better prepared for an actual regulatory audit. In addition, preparing for such a review allows a hedge fund to correct potential compliance deficiencies noted during the review prior to having a regulatory agency review them. Another common benefit after undergoing a mock audit is that afterwards, the hedge fund often uses the information gained as a result of the audit to assist in compliance planning. As many compliance consultants employ individuals who have worked previously at financial regulators, they are often familiar with the intricacies of what a hedge fund might actually experience during a regulatory audit.

On the other hand, some hedge funds may object to the process of engaging a third-party compliance consultant to perform these mock audits. Common objections cited include the expense and time necessary to undergo the process. Some hedge funds with large in-house compliance staff opt to perform these types of audits themselves as opposed to having a third party perform these reviews.

There is debate in the industry as to how frequently these audits need to be updated. Some argue that there is a benefit to only having additional future mock audits performed when a material change has occurred at the hedge fund that would present new compliance challenges that require a new review. Others believe that it is valuable to perform these mock audits with predetermined regularity, such as every three years, regardless as to whether or not any material changes have occurred at the hedge fund.

Differing scope of mock audits
There is no a single uniform approach utilized by compliance consultants to perform a mock audit. The services offered under the mock audit umbrella

range from a complete simulated audit to a more limited review focused for example to analyze a hedge fund's compliance documentation.

A simulated full regulatory audit often seeks to replicate the three common stages of real regulatory audits. The first stage involves the collection of documentation. The second stage involves conducting an on-site with the fund manager to review systems and additional documentation, as well as to conduct interviews with key personnel. The final stage involves reviewing the findings with the hedge fund and correcting any deficiencies noted during the mock audit.

The first stage—document collection—is often one of the more resource intensive parts of the process and merits further discussion. During this phase, a hedge fund typically receives a documentation request from the regulator. When a mock audit is performed, a compliance consultant works with the hedge fund to simulate this regulatory document request process.

In some cases, a hedge fund may not have already created a document that comports with the type or format commonly requested by regulators. In these cases, the compliance consultant works with the hedge fund to prepare these documents. After the review is complete the compliance consultant works to develop a method to store commonly requested documentation in an easy-to-organize format so that it is readily available to respond to regulatory inquiries.

The list of documentation commonly requested by regulators can be quite extensive and covers a wide variety of topics related to various aspects of a hedge fund's business, ranging from the investment performance of the funds under review to service provider contact information. Turning to the compliance-related documents common in regulatory requests, they, too, cover a broad spectrum of compliance topics, ranging from copies of compliance manuals to cybersecurity plans and client disclosure documentation.

What follows are some of the more commonly requested documents by the SEC during a routine examination, which are also commonly simulated by compliance consultants conducting mock reviews. This list is similar to that utilized by other financial regulators in major hedge fund jurisdictions around the world. When reviewing this list, it is helpful to consider not only which specific documents are being requested but also the compliance infrastructure and protocols necessary to support the information contained within these documents:

I. General Information
   1. Hedge fund's organization chart showing ownership percentages of the management company, control persons, and a schedule of all affiliated entities.

2. List of current employees, partners, officers, and directors, including their titles, office location, and hire date.
3. List of any employees, partners, officers, and directors who resigned or were terminated during the audit examination period and information regarding the reason for their departure.
4. List of any employees of the hedge fund who filed complaints against the firm or its employees, alleging potential violations of securities laws as the cause of the resignation or termination.
5. Any threatened, pending, and settled litigation or arbitration involving the hedge fund or any so-called persons related to the individual's association with the hedge fund or a securities-related matter, including a description of the allegations, the status, and a brief description of any settlements.
6. Standard client advisory contacts or agreements.
7. List of any subadvisers and accompanying agreements.
8. A list of all internal committees maintained. Include a description of each committee's responsibilities, frequency of meeting, a list of members of each committee, and clarify whether minutes of the meetings are taken.
9. The Form ADV Part 2B furnished to clients and any disclosure document used in conjunction with or in lieu of Part 2B.
10. The names and location of all key service providers and the services they perform.
11. Current fee schedules(s), if not otherwise stated in advisory contracts or in Form ADV Part II.
12. Any power of attorney obtained from clients.
13. Names of any joint ventures or any other businesses in which the hedge fund or any officer, director, portfolio manager, or trader participates or has any interest (other than their employment with the hedge fund), including a description of each relationship.

II. Information Regarding the Hedge Fund's Compliance Program, Risk Management, and Internal Controls

14. All compliance and operational policies in effect during the examination period.
15. Information relating to the hedge fund's testing of compliance including any internal control analyses, forensic, surveillance, or transactional tests performed by the firm.
16. A current inventory of the hedge fund's compliance risks that forms the basis for its policies and procedures, including any changes made to the inventory and the dates of the changes.
17. Any internal audit review schedules and completed audits, including the subject and the date of the report.

18. Written guidance that hedge fund has provided to its employees regarding its compliance risk assessment and documentation of compliance training during the audit examination period.
19. A list of all client complaints and information and associated correspondence.
20. A record of any noncompliance with the hedge fund's compliance policies and procedures. Detail any action taken as a result of these violations.
21. Information about the oversight process used to ensure compliance in remote offices.
22. Documentation maintained regarding any reviews conducted of the hedge fund's policies and procedures, including any annual and/or interim reports.

III. Information Processing, Reporting, and Protection
23. The Code of Ethics and insider trading policies and procedures.
24. If not included in the Code of Ethics, detail policies and procedures adopted to address:
    a. exemptions for employees
    b. personal trading
25. Reports of securities transactions reported by access persons.
26. If not stated in policies and procedures, information about the process used to monitor and control the receipt, flow, and use of nonpublic information.
27. Any fee-splitting or revenue-sharing arrangements.
28. Documentation of controls of employee access to physical locations containing customer information.
29. Documentation of electronic access controls, including user authorization and authentication, firewall configuration, security advisories on vulnerabilities in software and hardware installation configurations, and implementing work-arounds, security patches and upgrades.
30. Business continuity plan.

IV. Valuation
31. Names of all pricing services, quotation services and externally acquired portfolio accounting systems used in the valuation process and information about whether they are paid in hard or soft dollars, or a combination.
32. Names of all fair-valued and illiquid securities held by clients, and a description of any fair value process employed, including any testing and results and all fair value reports prepared or reviewed by a valuation committee.

33. Supporting documentation for the most recent advisory fee calculation, including performance fees and the manner in which the fees were calculated.

V. Information to Facilitate Testing with Respect to Advisory Trading Activities

34. A trade blotter (i.e., purchases and sales journal) that lists transactions (including all trade errors and reallocations) in securities and other financial instruments.

VI. Portfolio Management

35. Minutes of investment and/or portfolio management committee meetings, if such committees exist and minutes are maintained.

36. Names of any publicly traded companies for which employees of the hedge fund or its affiliates serve as officers and/or directors, and the name(s) of such employees.

37. Names of companies for which employees or the hedge fund or its affiliates serve on creditors' committees, and the name(s) of such employees.

VII. Fund Governance

38. Identify any relationship that the hedge fund or its affiliates maintained with any service provider. Provide documentation demonstrating that these service provider relationships were disclosed to the fund's board in connection with its review of the service provider contract. An example of this would be whether a fund has investments in the service provider.

39. Information regarding any compensation, whether direct or indirect, received by the hedge fund from any service providers. If compensation was received, provide documentation demonstrating that it was disclosed to the fund board of directors.

VIII. Brokerage Arrangements

40. Any documents created in the evaluation of brokerage arrangements and best execution.

41. Soft-dollar budgets or similar document that describes the products and services the hedge fund obtains using clients' brokerage commissions.

42. Commission-sharing arrangements, including the name of the broker-dealer and total dollars allocated to each arrangement during the examination period.

43. All affiliated broker-dealers, including a description of the affiliation and of their clearing arrangements.

44. Securities in which the hedge fund or an affiliate was a market maker.

IX. Performance Advertising and/or Marketing
The information described below is requested in order to facilitate testing of compliance with respect to advertising, marketing, and performance claims.

45. All pitchbooks, one-on-one presentations, pamphlets, brochures, and any other promotional and/or marketing materials furnished to existing and/or prospective clients for each investment strategy and/or mandate.

46. All advertisements used to inform or solicit clients. If information on services and investments is available on the Internet, such as websites and blogs, make all versions available as either printouts or electronic archives.

47. If the firm maintains websites, include sections for clients or advisory representatives that are accessible only with a username and password, please establish a temporary username and password for the staff's use during the inspection and include them in your responses.

48. All performance return composites, including description and investment objective, inception date, inclusion criteria such as account minimums, and whether they are used in marketing.

49. All parties compensated for soliciting clients or investors to affiliated private investment vehicles, including total cash and noncash compensation paid and a summary of the business relationship with that entity (e.g., consulting, prime brokerage, securities lending).

50. All requests for proposals (RFPs) completed.

51. Names of all third-party consultants that the hedge fund provided responses to questionnaires.

X. Fund Documentation
For each private fund, please provide the following:

52. Organization document and operating agreement (e.g., partnership agreement).

53. Financials, audited or unaudited, for its two most recent fiscal year ends.

54. General ledger, separated by calendar year, underlying the above-referenced statements.

55. Organizational chart of the general partner/managing member.

56. Account statements sent to investors during the current fiscal year, if any.

57. Names of current investors, including total current value of each investor's equity interest in the fund.

58. Names of investors who purchased and redeemed an interest in the fund during the examination period.
59. Latest advisory fee calculation, including any performance fee calculations, and the specific manner in which the fees were calculated.
60. A complete description of all positions held in side pockets or special situation accounts together with their valuation on the date of the related calculation of net asset values.
61. Side agreements/arrangements in which investors are participants. Please provide a description for each agreement/ arrangement.
62. If an entity, other than the hedge fund, maintains records regarding the interests of each fund investor in the fund, please request that entity to provide a confirmation of the following:
    a. Total number of shares outstanding if fund is in corporate form.
    b. Total number of limited partners.
    c. Most recently calculated value of each limited partner's interest in the fund.

CHAPTER SUMMARY

We began by introducing the different ways a hedge fund's service providers assist in the compliance process. Different ways to classify the compliance offerings of service providers such as fund administrators and auditors were discussed. We next turned to the role of specialized compliance consultants and the reasons for the increased growth in their use by hedge funds. The different services offered by compliance consultants was next discussed. This discussion included the use of consultants as outsourced CCOs. The pros and cons of outsourced CCO models was outlined as well as SEC survey data on best practices in this area. Finally, the role of compliance consultants in conducting mock regulatory audits was discussed with a focus on the document collection phase of the process.

Now that we have developed a basic understanding of the role of documentation in the regulatory audit process, in the next chapter, we will return to this subject and focus in more detail on key hedge fund compliance documentation.

NOTE

1. National Exam Program Risk Alert, "Examination of Advisers and Funds That Outsource Their Chief Compliance Officers," vol. 5, no. 1 (November 9, 2015).

CHAPTER 7

Understanding Key Compliance Documentation

REASONS FOR DOCUMENTING COMPLIANCE POLICIES AND PROCEDURES

The previous chapters have established a framework for understanding hedge fund compliance. This has included a discussion of core areas of hedge fund compliance and the role of service providers in supporting the function. However, we have not directly addressed the documentation of these policies. There are several reasons why the documentation of compliance is critical, including:

- *Documentation required by regulators*—Depending on the jurisdiction(s) in which they are located, hedge funds may be required by regulators to develop and maintain compliance documentation. An example of this would be a U.S.-registered hedge fund required by the U.S. Securities and Exchange Commission to maintain a compliance manual.
- *Enhanced communication of compliance practices to employees*—Every hedge fund's compliance program is unique. In addition to verbally explaining all policies to its employees, documenting the policies in writing is another way to enhance communication of the policies and practices in place.
- *Road map for oversight by hedge fund management and service providers*—Compliance policies and their implementation at hedge funds are often subject to oversight not only by compliance personnel, such as the CCO, but by other individuals as well. These individuals typically include senior management that are not focused directly on the compliance function, such as the Chief Investment Officer and Chief Operating Officer. In addition, certain service providers, such as compliance consultants and fund directors, may also need to provide

oversight of a hedge fund's compliance program. Having these policies in writing as opposed to in an oral format facilitates this oversight.

■ *Enhanced communication of compliance practices to investors*—The due diligence process of prospective investors often includes a review of a hedge fund's compliance program. Having written documentation of policies and procedures facilitates this analysis. In addition, existing investors may seek to monitor changes in a hedge fund's compliance program as part of their ongoing due diligence. Written documentation also facilitates this oversight by providing reference documentation.

■ *Facilitation of change management*—Compliance policies and practices at hedge funds evolve over time. By creating a written record of a hedge fund's program, the updating of records creates an ongoing archive by which the changes can be monitored.

UNDERSTANDING THE GOALS OF COMPLIANCE DOCUMENTATION

Now that we have outlined some of the reasons for a hedge fund to develop written compliance documentation, we can next turn to the issue of what the goals should be in developing the content of compliance documentation. Key goals typically include the following:

■ *Minimum regulatory compliance*—As is a recurring theme in many areas of hedge fund compliance, one of the goals of compliance documentation is to comply with minimum regulatory requirements. For example, U.S. SEC Rule 206(4)-7(b) the Investment Advisors Act of 1940 (Advisers Act) outlines that entities known as Investment Advisers, such as hedge funds, must conduct an annual review of their policies to ensure *"the adequacy of the policies and procedures established pursuant to this section and the effectiveness of their implementation."*

If a registered hedge fund therefore does not document that it will perform this annual review of its policies and perform the review in actuality, then they are not operating in compliance with the regulatory guidance in this area. The language covering these types of minimum regulatory requirements are often contained in what is called the *compliance manual*, which is a document that provides an overview of compliance policies and procedures. While typically not a hedge fund's only compliance document, it is the cornerstone of its compliance program.

■ *Demonstrative documentation*—A second goal of compliance documentation is to outline the actual compliance practices in place. By outlining specific steps that employees at the firm should take to comply with policies in its compliance documents, a hedge fund will set out a clear path by which employees may be in compliance. An example would be the specific forms, be they hard copy or preferably electronic in nature, that employees may utilize to facilitate approvals by the compliance department, such as a personal trading preclearance form. Examples of these types of forms are often found in appendixes to other compliance documents, such as the compliance manual. In addition, in recent years there has been a trend for hedge funds to maintain copies of demonstrative documentation on intranets or internal websites for ease of access.

JURISDICTIONAL DIFFERENCES IN COMPLIANCE DOCUMENTATION

As we have discussed throughout this book, hedge funds operate in multiple jurisdictions throughout the world. Due to different regulations and laws in different countries, certain elements of compliance documentation may be different in different regions. For example, a hedge fund in Hong Kong will have certain compliance-specific requirements that are different than a hedge fund in the United Kingdom, and the documentation will reflect this. For hedge funds that operate in multiple jurisdictions, a situation could arise in which two different compliance manuals may even be in place in each jurisdiction. In that case, the employees in each jurisdiction would typically be subject to the local compliance manual or policies in effect in their particular office for jurisdiction-specific compliance requirements, and broader firm-wide compliance policies for areas that were not mandated by local regulators.

While these jurisdictional differences are reflected in the relevant compliance documentation, certain elements of all compliance programs are agnostic. That is, regardless of the regulatory requirements in place in different countries, certain elements of compliance programs are universal in their nature. For example, whether a hedge fund is in the United States or in Singapore, it is considered best practice for both to implement a personal account dealing oversight program. While the regulatory requirements surrounding these programs may be different, the presence of such a program in the compliance documentation should be the same.

UNDERSTANDING BOILERPLATE DOCUMENTATION

An important concept as it relates to core hedge fund compliance documentation is what is known as *boilerplate documentation*. Boilerplate documentation is generic off-the-shelf documentation, or sections of documents, that have been prepared in advance and are not specific to any one hedge fund. The use of boilerplate documentation is common in the industry. Two of the more frequent areas in which this type of documentation is utilized are in compliance and legal documentation.

A common legal and compliance-related document in which boilerplate language is found is a hedge fund's offering memorandum. An *offering memorandum*, or OM, is a legal document used to present a detailed overview of a particular fund's strategy, personnel, and risks. Funds are required to present investors with an OM, along with other documents, prior to making an investment in a fund. They are often quite long and may exceed 200 pages. OMs are essentially a collection of a series of disclosures and policy descriptions that facilitate the mutual understanding and contract between a hedge fund investor and the fund manager as to how the fund will be managed and the rights and obligations of the different parties. OMs differ from marketing documentation, such as a hedge fund's due diligence questionnaire or marketing presentations, in that the OM is often written in a technical legal matter. To this end, OMs are often replete with legal disclaimers and boilerplate sections of specific language that have special legal implications.

The primary reasons for the use of boilerplate documentation and language in compliance documents are twofold. First, in many instances, there is no reason to re-create the wheel. Over the years, the industry has developed certain standard document formats that have proved over time to comply with common industry practices and legal and regulatory requirements. Second, hedge funds realize a cost savings in using boilerplate documentation. Rather than, for example, hiring a compliance consultant or a law firm to draft a compliance manual from scratch, the hedge fund can leverage off the existing work of the service provider and theoretically reduce their costs. In practice, many service providers will utilize this boilerplate documentation as a starting point to develop specific compliance documents for their clients.

Risks of Boilerplate Documentation

From a compliance perspective, on its face there is nothing wrong with utilizing boilerplate documentation as a starting point in drafting compliance documentation. That being said, the use of this documentation also presents a number of risks:

- *Overly generic or vague documentation*—One of the key risks in utilizing this boilerplate documentation is that hedge funds face the temptation of effectively purchasing compliance documents from service providers and not customizing them as appropriate to the compliance practices in place at the hedge fund. This can create a disconnect for employees, investors, and regulators. If boilerplate compliance documentation is overly generic, it will not provide specific enough compliance guidance for employees. Similarly, those external to the hedge fund, such as investors seeking to analyze the compliance program, will not find this documentation useful for compliance analyses. Finally, if regulators discover that compliance practices described in documentation are not being followed, it can create issues for the hedge fund, which may lead the regulator to take corrective action, including sanctions and fines.

- *Too-specific incorrect documentation*—In certain instances, boilerplate documentation may be written to accommodate large hedge funds. This creates a problem when a smaller or newly formed hedge fund seeks to utilize this off-the-shelf boilerplate documentation. One of the biggest problems using such broad boilerplate documents is that they often discuss practices not in place at the smaller hedge funds or that are too robust in nature to be appropriate for smaller funds.

To demonstrate the differences between the usage of vague boilerplate and language that is too specific, let us consider a document we discussed in Chapter 5 known as a *business continuity plan* (BCP), or a *business continuity and disaster recovery plan (BCP/DR)*, which are contingency plans that allow a hedge fund to continue operations in the event of business disruption or disaster event.

Let us consider the problem of too-specific boilerplate language first. Assume that the boilerplate document outlines that a hedge fund must test its BCP/DR plans biannually and formally document the results. While such frequent testing is appropriate in a larger hedge fund, in a small hedge fund of, say, three people, that does not maintain an in-house information technology function, the firm's employees may not be equipped to perform such tests, or, alternatively, they may informally perform them without documenting them properly. For this smaller hedge fund, this policy would be inaccurate as compared to the actual compliance practices in place at the firm. While it would be certainly advisable for the smaller fund to test its BCP/DR plans more frequently, this is not what is happening in practice. This difference between the compliance policies described in a fund's documentation and the actual compliance practices in place is known as the *policy/practice gap*.

Next, we can turn to the problem of vague boilerplate language. If a hedge fund's compliance manual stated that BCP plans should be tested on a regular basis, it may be unclear how frequently that is, which can lead to confusion. In practice, a hedge fund may test the plans every year, but others reading the manual, perhaps regulators or prospective investors, may interpret a regular basis to be as frequently as twice a year. This type of confusion may also lead to problems with financial regulators who may interpret the term *regularly* to mean more frequently than a hedge fund is actually testing its plans.

In summary, the use of boilerplate documentation by hedge funds and their service providers in developing compliance documentation is not inherently an ill-advised practice as a starting point. The key is that the boilerplate documentation should then be customized to reflect the actual policies and procedures in place at the hedge fund and thus eliminate the policy/practice gap.

CORE COMPLIANCE DOCUMENTATION

We can now begin to address key compliance documentation in more detail. A hedge fund has a series of compliance documents that constitute the outline of its compliance program. To be clear, as we have outlined throughout this book, a hedge fund compliance program consists of much more than simply a series of documents. The compliance rules, guidelines, and practices described in the documentation must actually be put into place. The documentation provides the blueprint by which the compliance program can be executed. Key compliance documents include:

- *Compliance manual*—The central document to a hedge fund's compliance program is the compliance manual. While the minimum regulatory requirements of compliance manuals differ across jurisdictions, there are certain compliance-related topics that are generally addressed in the majority of compliance manuals. The following example table of contents of a compliance manual demonstrates the wide range of topics typically covered in compliance manuals:

TABLE OF CONTENTS

I. Introduction
II. Identification of chief compliance officer and supervised persons
III. Compliance policies and procedures:
    A. Disclosures and risk assessments
    B. Contracts

C. Portfolio management processes
D. Trading and brokerage practices
E. Valuation
F. Fees
G. Insider trading prevention
H. Safeguarding of client assets
I. Media relations
J. Advertising and marketing
K. Use of third-party marketers
L. Privacy policy and protecting client information
M. Proxy voting
N. Conflicts of interests
O. Business continuity and disaster recovery
P. Books and records
Q. Electronic communications policy
R. Complaints and rumors
S. Business entertainment
T. Political contributions
U. Oversight of third-party service providers

IV. Annual review of policies and procedures

■ *Code of ethics*—The code of ethics, which is sometimes referred to as a *code of conduct,* is a document that summarizes key aspects of a hedge fund's compliance program. The code of ethics, as opposed to the compliance manual, is traditionally less technical and written in a more user-friendly format for employees' use. In addition, code of ethics documents may contain more specific details regarding the actual practices employed by a particular hedge fund in certain areas rather than the more technical regulatory descriptions contained in compliance manuals. A hedge fund may also decide to combine their compliance manual and code of ethics into a single document.

■ *Other compliance documentation*—Hedge funds may address certain issues in a compliance manual on a high level and then may develop stand-alone manuals to delve into more detail in certain topics. These stand-alone policies can focus on a variety of different topics. Examples of common stand-alone policies include:

■ *Best execution policy*—The concept of best execution refers to a hedge fund's ability to seek the execution of trades for its investors under favorable terms. Hedge funds generally consider a number of terms when evaluating best execution of their trades, including execution price, speed, and quality, as well as any additional benefits to the hedge fund from utilizing particular brokers for execution such as industry- or company-specific research. Considering the qualitative nature of some of the factors that may be evaluated, there is often a degree of discretion that hedge funds afford themselves in designing their compliance policies in this area. The following example excerpt of language from a best execution policy demonstrates the wide variety of factors that go into analyzing best execution and a common process by which a hedge fund may seek to evaluate it.

The hedge fund has an obligation to seek best execution of clients' transactions under the circumstances of the particular transaction. To fulfill this duty, this hedge fund must execute securities transactions for clients in such a manner that the client's total cost or proceeds in each transaction is the most favorable under the circumstances.

Best execution is determined on a trade-by-trade basis and should result in the best qualitative execution, not necessarily the best possible commission cost. A key element of the duty of best execution is obtaining the best price at which securities transaction are executed. Best price is considered to be the highest price that a client can sell a security and the lowest price that a client can purchase a security. Other components of best execution are securing low commission rates for clients, as well as timeliness of having a transaction executed by a broker, the value of research provided, the responsiveness of the broker to the hedge fund, and the financial responsibility of the broker.

Typically, to achieve best execution, a hedge fund may aggregate or batch client orders. If aggregation of trading is not utilized or available, the hedge fund is required to disclose to clients that it will not aggregate transactions and the fact that clients may pay higher commissions as a result.

At least annually, selected employees of the hedge fund will meet to evaluate systematically the execution performance of its brokers. The review of brokers will consist of various factors, including:

- The services provided by the broker other than execution, including research or brokerage services and products;
- Average commission rate charged by each broker;

- Potential conflicts of interest (such as directing brokerage to a broker who makes client referrals to the hedge fund);
- The value of research provided by each broker;
- Whether the execution and other services provided by the broker were satisfactory considering factors that include the speed of execution and the ability to handle large orders; and
- The reason for using that broker such as for research purposes or only for the purposes of execution.

- *Soft-dollar policies*—Soft dollars refer to commission credits from brokers on trades executed by hedge funds. These credits are paid back to hedge funds from brokers in exchange for their business. It is legal, in most instances, for hedge funds to receive these credits and to utilize them for certain brokerage and research services. In order to ensure that soft dollars are utilized appropriately for the benefit of a hedge fund's clients and in a consistent manner across all clients, hedge funds generally maintain written soft-dollar policies.

The use of soft dollars may also create a potential for a conflict of interest for a hedge fund. The following example excerpt from a soft-dollar policy highlights this potential conflict and the ways in which a compliance program can take measures to minimize these conflicts and oversee a hedge fund's use of soft dollars.

The hedge fund's use of client commissions to obtain research and brokerage services creates a conflict of interest. For example, the hedge fund will not have to pay for the research and brokerage services. This creates a potential incentive for the hedge fund to select a broker to execute transactions based on the hedge fund's interests in obtaining the research or brokerage services, rather than the interest of the client in paying the lowest possible commission rate. The following procedures have been adopted by the hedge fund to address this conflict.

A. Approval Process:
   1. All requests for payment with soft dollars must be approved by the Chief Compliance Officer (CCO). Any contracts or other

(Continued)

written agreements as well as a description of the purpose of the payment should be included with the request.

2. The Compliance Officer will consult with the hedge fund's Head Trader regarding the capabilities of brokers and will determine whether the particular service qualifies as an eligible research or brokerage service

B. Criteria for Approval:

A number of criteria are to be considered in approving soft-dollar allocations, including the broker-dealer's business reputation and financial position, the ability to execute orders in a cost-effective and professional manner, and the manner in which they prepare timely and accurate trade confirmations and provide research services to the hedge fund.

The hedge fund has an obligation to obtain best execution of investors' transactions. Therefore, no allocation for soft-dollar payments shall be made unless best execution of the transaction is expected to be obtained.

C. Quarterly Reports/Broker Statements:

1. The Head Trader will generate periodic reports of commission use. These reports will be reviewed by the CCO. For each broker that has received commissions on trades, the report will show the total amount of commissions and soft-dollar commissions paid.

2. These reports will be compared to soft-dollar summaries generated by the broker-dealers themselves in order to determine whether there were any discrepancies.

■ *Trade allocation policy*—Trade allocation refers to the process by which a hedge fund allocates the investments it purchases among the different funds it manages. To ensure a consistent and equitable allocation of investments among the firm's funds, hedge funds traditionally maintain trade allocation policies. Where practical, most hedge funds strive to allocate investments on a pro-rata basis. The following is an example excerpt of a section of a trade allocation policy demonstrating how hedge funds typically allocate trades.

The hedge fund must ensure that, when aggregating and allocating securities transactions, clients are treated in a fair and equitable manner.

The hedge fund manages numerous accounts and consequently must utilize an established methodology for allocating securities. Investment decisions frequently affect more than one account and sometimes more than one type of account. It is therefore inevitable that at times it will be desirable to acquire or dispose of the same security for more than one client account at the same time. The fund's policy is to equitably allocate and buy and sell executions among clients when feasible. To the extent that a portfolio manager seeks to acquire the same security at the same time for more than one client account, it may not be possible to acquire or sell a sufficiently large quantity of the security, or the price at which the security is obtained for clients or different funds may vary.

Procedures for Portfolio Managers for Trade Aggregation and Allocation:

1. Portfolio managers are primarily responsible for making trade aggregation and allocation decisions in accordance with this policy.

2. Prior to including an account in a trade, the portfolio manager is required to determine that the trade is appropriate and permitted for each account that will participate, and that the hedge fund will receive no additional compensation as a result.

3. The portfolio manager and the trader(s) will maintain precise books and records for each trade aggregation and allocation.

- *Trade error policy*—Throughout the course of its investment and trading activities, hedge funds will occasionally be involved in trading errors. In some instances, these errors may be the fault of the hedge fund, in other cases third parties such as trading counterparties may be at fault. Hedge funds maintain trade error policies so that these errors are handled in a consistent manner and do not unfairly disadvantage clients. The following example excerpt is demonstrative of language commonly contained in trade error policies.

Trading errors must be corrected as soon as possible upon discovery. The following procedures should be followed to properly handle trading errors. Failure to follow these procedures may result in compounding the error and greater expense to the hedge fund.

1. All material trade errors must be documented. The CCO will maintain copies of the completed trade error report for monitoring, reimbursement, and regulatory purposes.

2. Determining Trade Error Amount and Correction Errors
   a. In determining whether a client has suffered a loss or missed an investment opportunity as a result of a trade error, the portfolio manager and management must determine the position the client would have been in, if the error had not occurred.
   b. The hedge fund's management will determine an appropriate method to correct an error in light of the facts and circumstances.

3. Prohibited Activity
   Under no circumstances may a trade executed in error for a particular client account be reallocated to another client's account unless such other client's preexisting order for the same security was not filled in its entirety.

4. Reporting Trade Errors to Managing Member and CCO
   a. The individual who commits a trade error, which results in a client or broker-dealer reimbursement, must notify the hedge fund's CCO immediately.
   b. The CCO will keep a record of all material trade errors that occur throughout the year and their impact.

■ *Anti-money laundering (AML) policy*—These policies are utilized to outline compliance policies and procedures with regard to the prevention investments in the hedge fund from being used to launder money which could be used for example to finance terrorist activities. Regulators in different jurisdictions increasingly mandate AML policies. In the United States, a recent proposal by the U.S. Treasury's Financial Crimes Enforcement Network (FinCEN) would require U.S.

SEC-registered investment advisers, including registered hedge funds, to establish more robust anti-money laundering programs.[1]

Even without the formal codification of these proposed rules, in practice, many hedge funds already maintain AML programs, and they are effectively managed by the fund administrators. For illustration, what follows is an example excerpt of language that would be contained in an AML policy that outlines this delegation. In reviewing this excerpt, notice the compliance obligation placed on the hedge fund's CCO to evaluate the service provider's due diligence on investors.

> The Hedge Fund Company (Company) may contract with administrators or other third-party service providers to assist the Company in complying with the policies and procedures set forth in its AML policy. If the Company has so contracted, each administrator or other third-party service provider shall execute a certification. In addition, the CCO shall evaluate the services provided by the administrator or third-party service provider to assess the effectiveness of this policy. This evaluation may include, among other things, a review of the due diligence process for new and prospective investors employed by the administrator or third-party service provider and the accuracy of the reporting mechanisms utilized.

Other common policies may include the following:

- Anti-Bribery Policy and Procedures
- Conflicts of Interest Policy
- Gifts and Entertainment Policy
- Market Rumors Policy
- Personal Account Dealing Policy
- Pay to Play Policy
- Proxy Voting Policy and Guidelines
- Whistle Blower and Anti-Retaliation Policy and Procedures
- Risk Policies
- Valuation Policies
- Custody Policy and Procedures
- Soliciting Prospective Investors Policy
- Privacy and Data Confidentiality Policy

In addition, other policies may focus on the compliance aspects of technology-related matters many of which were introduced in Chapter 5. Examples of those policies include the following:

- Data Backup Policy
- Cybersecurity Policy
- Social Networking Policy
- Telephone and Electronic Communications Recording Policy
- Business Continuity and Disaster Recovery Plan

Jurisdiction-Specific Compliance Policies

Certain jurisdictions or regulators may require that a hedge fund maintain specific policies as well. To ensure compliance with applicable jurisdictional regulations, a hedge fund may choose to develop a stand-alone policy rather than place the policy inside a larger document, such as an offering memorandum or compliance manual.

An example of a common stand-alone policy is the effective requirement for the majority of European hedge funds under the Alternative Investment Fund Managers Directive (AIFMD) to maintain Remuneration Policies. Similarly, hedge funds that manage money on behalf of institutions subject to the U.S. Employee Retirement Income Security Act of 1974 (ERISA) are required to maintain ERISA Monitoring Policies. While it is not uncommon to find language addressing ERISA monitoring in a hedge fund's offering memorandum, a hedge fund may also maintain a stand-alone policy to address the more technical aspects of this issue.

In some instances, a hedge fund may decide not to develop a separate standalone manual to cover these topics at all, but rather may simply incorporate them in detail into the larger compliance manual. Ultimately, it generally makes no difference as long as the subject matter is appropriately documented from a compliance perspective.

The Role of Compliance in Influencing Other Noncompliance Documents

In addition to documentation primarily centered around compliance policies and procedures, hedge funds also maintain a number of other documents not as focused on compliance. Common examples of these documents include:

- Due diligence questionnaire
- Marketing presentations (sometimes referred to as pitchbooks)
- Audited financial statements

- Client reporting
- Operations manuals
- Investment research memoranda

While not being pure compliance documents, these documents are certainly influenced by the compliance policies in place. In addition, many if not all of these documents are often subject to some degree of oversight by the compliance and legal functions as well. For example, consider a marketing presentation. There are often a number of required disclaimers that these documents are required to maintain. The compliance department, in conjunction with the legal department, depending on the structure of the hedge funds resources in this area, is often tasked with ensuring that the appropriate disclaimers are in place.

Similarly, it may be the job of compliance to ensure that certain documentation is produced on an ongoing basis. For example, when making a change in an investment recommendation, a hedge fund may have a compliance policy that outlines that a new internal investment memorandum must be produced each time a hedge fund changes its valuation assumptions regarding holdings it prices. These are referred to as *manager marked positions*. In some cases, the investment team may discuss the change and approve it, but may simply forget to produce the required memorandum documenting the change. This is where compliance would step in not only to remind the investment personnel to produce the memo, but also to ensure that it is in the proper format and contains the appropriate information to reflect the change. As the examples above highlight, despite the fact that a particular document may not be solely focused on compliance-related matters, it may still be influenced and subject to oversight by the compliance function.

CHAPTER SUMMARY

We began by outlining the key reasons why compliance needs to be documented. These reasons include regulatory requirements, unique differences among hedge fund compliance programs, and the facilitation of the ongoing management of changes to compliance policies. Next, we proceeded to discuss the goals of compliance documentation, including complying with regulatory guidelines and providing written compliance guidelines for employees. We then addressed topics relating to jurisdictional differences in compliance documentation and the use of boilerplate templates in developing compliance documents. Finally, we addressed the development of stand-alone policy manuals to address specific areas of compliance, and the role of the compliance function in addressing noncompliance documents.

In the next chapter, we will discuss the ways in which a hedge fund's prospective and existing investors evaluate and monitor compliance functions. As part of this process, they collect and review many of the compliance documents discussed in this chapter.

NOTE

1. U.S. Department of the Treasury Financial Crimes Enforcement Network, "Federal Register Notices: Anti-Money Laundering Program and Suspicious Activity Report Filing Requirements for Registered Investment Advisers, Notice of Proposed Rulemaking," August 2015.

CHAPTER 8

Investor Evaluation of Hedge Fund Compliance Functions

INTRODUCTION

In previous chapters, our discussion of hedge fund compliance practices has primarily been from the perspective of the hedge fund manager. In this chapter, we shift focus to investors seeking to evaluate hedge fund compliance functions. Hedge funds maintain a certain amount of discretion regarding the specific ways in which they implement their compliance programs. As such, the specific details regarding the implementation of compliance programs are not universally consistent among hedge funds. As a result of these differences it is important for investors to not assume all hedge fund compliance programs are created equal.

Hedge fund investors come in two primary forms. The first group are *prospective investors* considering making an investment, sometimes referred to as an allocation or the commitment of capital, to a hedge fund. The second group are *existing investors* who have already committed capital to a hedge fund. For the purposes of this discussion, the term *investors* will be utilized to refer to both prospective and existing investors.

COMPLIANCE EVALUATIONS IN INVESTOR DUE DILIGENCE

Both prospective and existing investors approach the subject of hedge fund compliance with a goal of evaluating the quality and strength of the oversight of the compliance function.

Evaluating a Culture of Compliance

Whether conducting initial or ongoing analysis of a hedge fund's compliance environment, investors seek to evaluate the quality of the overall compliance environment. It is difficult sometimes to define a qualitative term like *quality* when seeking to make a detailed due diligence evaluation of the compliance function. Effectively, investors seek to gauge whether a culture of compliance is in place; however, this, too, is a vague notion that is difficult to specifically evaluate. In practice, the specific elements investors traditionally look for when evaluating the culture of the compliance at a hedge fund include:

- Strength of compliance controls
- Appropriateness of resources devoted to the compliance function
- Frequency and comprehensiveness of compliance training
- Independence of the compliance function
- Robustness of ongoing compliance oversight and testing
- Presence of a history of any violations of internal compliance policies or regulatory violations

The Larger Due Diligence Processes

The evaluation of the compliance function is often part of a larger evaluative process known as *due diligence*. Due diligence is broadly split into two types. The first is *investment due diligence* (IDD), which focuses primarily on the investment-related aspects of the hedge funds. The second category is *operational due diligence* (ODD), and it focuses primarily on non-investment-related aspects of a fund's management. The evaluation of the compliance function of a hedge fund is traditionally rooted more heavily in ODD as opposed to IDD; however, there is overlap among the two areas.

When an investor approaches a compliance evaluation, they traditionally do not do so in isolation. A stand-alone review is not generally conducted only of the compliance function itself, but rather the review is part of the larger due diligence process, which covers a wide variety of compliance-related issues.

Many of these other areas covered during the larger due diligence process, while not directly part of the compliance function, have compliance elements or directly overlap with compliance. An example of such overlap would be an analysis of a hedge fund's operational controls surrounding valuation procedures. While it is tempting to perhaps refer to this as the so-called valuation section of the due diligence review, there are certainly a number of compliance-related elements associated with the fund valuation process, such as evaluating how the compliance function of the hedge fund oversees compliance with the number of pricing sources utilized as may be required by the firm's valuation policies.

INITIAL AND ONGOING COMPLIANCE ANALYSIS

The main difference between existing and prospective investor evaluations of a hedge fund's compliance function relates to the timing and goals of the due diligence process. Specifically, there are two primary goals for the investor evaluation:

1. *Initial compliance analysis*—An investor analyzes a hedge fund's compliance function for the first time.
2. *Ongoing compliance monitoring*—An investor performs continued evaluations of a hedge fund's compliance function after an initial review has been completed.

While they may perform due diligence on other aspects of a hedge fund, some investors choose to ignore best practices and perform little or no due diligence on the compliance function prior to investing. The reasons for this can include a historical lack of focus on compliance due diligence for a particular investor, a lack of resources, and a lack of specialized knowledge required to evaluate the compliance function. While certainly not advisable, this could result in a situation, whereby an existing investor, realizing the error of their ways in not performing initial due diligence, could decide several years after making an investment in a hedge fund to analyze the compliance function for the first time. This special case, therefore, would be considered initial compliance analysis for an existing investor rather than ongoing monitoring.

It is important to distinguish between initial analysis and ongoing monitoring because they are often on different time lines and require different allocations of resources from investors. Additionally, there are often slightly different goals associated with the two different stages of compliance analysis. In the next section, we will address these differences in our discussion of the process by which investors actually analyze hedge fund compliance functions.

Stages of Initial Compliance Analysis

The process an investor follows to conduct an initial compliance analysis can be broadly categorized into three stages:

> *Stage 1: Collect and review compliance documentation*—To begin the initial analysis of the compliance function, an investor starts by collecting documentation from a hedge fund. The documents collected

are the compliance policies and procedures described in the previous chapter, and should include key compliance documentation, such as the compliance manual and code of ethics as applicable.

After this documentation is collected from the hedge fund, an investor would then proceed to review it and develop an initial understanding of the hedge fund's compliance function. As compliance evaluations are typically conducted as part of the larger due diligence process, there may be other additional documents that are reviewed that cover a wide variety of topics, such as a hedge fund's marketing pitchbook or due diligence questionnaire; these other documents can often provide valuable insights into compliance practices and procedures.

Stage 2: Conduct interviews with compliance personnel—After the appropriate documentation has been collected and reviewed, an investor would next proceed to conduct an interview with compliance personnel. These interviews serve two primary functions. First, they afford an investor with the opportunity to confirm the information outlined in the collected documentation. Second, they allow investors to fill in any gaps in their understanding of a hedge fund's compliance program, as well as gain additional insights into the function of compliance programs. If possible, it is considered a best practice for an investor to conduct these interviews in person and onsite in the hedge fund manager's office.

One benefit of conducting an in-person interview is that it provides the opportunity for an investor to review additional compliance documentation directly in the hedge fund manager's office. In certain instances, citing primarily confidentiality concerns, a hedge fund may only provide investors with limited excerpts or the table of contents of certain compliance documentation that they may have requested. For example, this is common practice with a hedge fund's compliance manual. To review the entire document an investor may be required to physically visit the fund manager's office and review it there. A second benefit to an in-person onsite interview is that an investor will also have the direct opportunity to review a demonstration of the hedge fund's compliance-related systems operating in practice. While not preferred, in certain instances, investors do not have the resources to visit a manager onsite, and instead opt to conduct these interviews remotely through a video conference or through screen-sharing technology.

Stage 3: Analyze and confirm compliance-related service provider relationships—Service providers can play a critical role in the compliance process. It is important that investors do not neglect analyzing these service providers when performing due diligence on the compliance function. The service provider review process can be categorized into three general stages:

1. *Relationship confirmation*—To ensure a hedge fund is not fraudulently fabricating its relationships with a particular compliance service provider, investors should first attempt to independently confirm that an actual relationship is in place.

2. *Document collection*—After the relationship is confirmed an investor would next proceed with collecting documentation from the service provider relevant to their relationship with the hedge fund. Examples of this could include marketing materials that provide an overview of the service provider's firm and service level agreements (SLAs) detailing the compliance services provided to the hedge fund.

3. *Interview*—After the relevant documentation has been collected and reviewed, an investor would next conduct an interview with the service provider. Similar to the interview conducted with the hedge fund, the goals of this interview are to confirm the information obtained in the documentation as well as to gain additional insights into the way the service provider works with the hedge fund's compliance function. While it is beneficial to conduct these meetings on site, it is common industry practice for investors to conduct these service provider meetings remotely through the phone or video conference in most cases.

Ongoing Compliance Monitoring

Once initial compliance monitoring is completed, investors should perform ongoing monitoring of a hedge fund in order to continually update their initial compliance due diligence.

Reasons for Performing Ongoing Compliance Monitoring A hedge fund's compliance challenges evolve over time. In order to ensure a hedge fund is meeting these challenges appropriately, after an initial evaluation is complete, an investor should seek to perform ongoing monitoring of the compliance function. From an investment perspective, the portfolio of a hedge fund today may have a significantly different composition than it did when an investor first allocated capital. Many hedge funds' operational environments change over time as well. These changes are a result of the normal growth of the hedge fund (i.e., as the fund raises more capital, it implements more robust operational systems) or instead driven by external changes (i.e., a new law is passed which requires the hedge fund to operate differently). These changes have compliance implications as well. Therefore, in addition to initial due diligence, existing investors in a fund need to perform ongoing compliance due diligence (i.e., postinvestment due diligence) on the hedge fund as well.

Stages of Ongoing Compliance Monitoring   The general steps in the ongoing compliance monitoring are the same as those in the initial compliance management process. One of the primary differences between the two processes is that by the ongoing monitoring stage, an investor will have already performed an initial compliance review to guide their efforts. The goal of the ongoing process is to build on that existing knowledge to reevaluate the hedge fund's current compliance environment. By leveraging this initial foundation, ongoing monitoring processes are usually less resource intensive and may require less time to complete.

Scheduling Ongoing Compliance Monitoring   The timing of ongoing compliance monitoring reviews is typically dependent on the frequency with which an investor updates their other due diligence on the hedge fund. In practice, many investors conduct at least annual due diligence updates of their hedge funds; however, in the event new circumstances or risks arise for the hedge fund on an intra-year basis that requires more frequent ongoing reviews, then investors would adjust their review processes accordingly to review these new items.

EVALUATING BEST PRACTICE COMPLIANCE

Throughout this book, we have focused primarily on aspects of hedge fund compliance that require adherence to law-based rules. The enforcement of these rules is implemented by regulators and associated groups, such as self-regulatory organizations. Investors performing due diligence on the compliance function are concerned not only about how a hedge fund minimally complies with these regulations, but also about how they may exceed them through *best practice compliance*.

Minimum Regulatory Compliance

When a legislature enacts a law, such as they did in the United States in 2010 with the passage of the Dodd-Frank Wall Street Reform and Consumer Protection Act (Dodd-Frank), these new rules become the law of the land. That is, if a fund manager, whether they are a hedge fund or any other type of manager, would like to legally conduct business after the passage of Dodd-Frank, and they were not exempt, they would need to comply with the law in order to legally operate their business. If a hedge fund manager does not follow the current law, then they are *out-of-compliance* and not operating legally.

Depending on the severity of their noncompliance, a fund manager operating out-of-compliance either can be sanctioned, fined, or ultimately shut down by regulators. Investors evaluating regulatory compliance at a hedge fund continually focus on the potential for a hedge fund to be out-of-compliance due to the negative consequences it can have for both the fund and its investors.

When a hedge fund seeks to specifically comply with the minimum legal requirements, including all of the current laws and regulations applicable to it, it is pursuing *minimum regulatory compliance*. This can be thought of as when a hedge fund follows the letter of the law and nothing else. This approach is also referred to as *law-based compliance*, or *rules-based compliance*.

Investors are increasingly focused on the ways in which a hedge fund not only meets minimum regulatory requirements but also exceeds them. Indeed, many hedge funds, if not all of them, go above and beyond these minimum levels of compliance. There are two key reasons for this:

1. *Regulatory guidance*—Beyond the pure legal requirements for minimum regulatory compliance, regulators often issue *guidance*. Guidance is additional information put out by regulators outlining the financial regulators' further interpretation and perspectives on laws and regulations that hedge funds should abide by.

   This guidance can be thought of as a gentle nudge by regulators to encourage funds not only to meet with minimum requirements, but also to go above them in order to pursue better practices. While these recommendations may not carry the same legal obligations as bright-line rules, they still hold some weight nonetheless.

   This guidance can come in many forms, including responses to inquiries from other regulated fund managers, public statements and speeches by regulatory personnel, testimony by regulatory officials to the legislature, and industry studies. As an example, the SEC provides guidance through avenues including webcasts, roundtables, forums, summits, and open meetings streamed over the Internet. Resources to access this guidance are available at www.sec.gov/news/webcasts .shtml. Another example of guidance are annual announcements by hedge fund regulators with regard to examination priorities, such as the type outlined in the United Kingdom's Financial Conduct Authority (FCA) annual business plans.[1]

2. *Investor feedback and pressure*—In addition to being legally required to adhere to minimum regulatory guidelines, hedge funds are ultimately accountable to their investors. In recent years, investors have increasingly devoted more resources toward performing due diligence on fund managers prior to investing.

If a hedge fund has a history of maintaining a weak compliance environment, has a history of problems or fines with regulators, or has an inefficient compliance function, investors may decide not to invest, no matter how compelling the investment opportunity is. Hedge funds understandably do not like this, and if enough investors do not invest, the hedge fund will either not grow or ultimately go out of business.

The combination of guidance by regulators encouraging funds to go beyond minimum requirements as well as enhanced investor scrutiny both prior to and after investing has created an environment in which hedge funds are practically forced to pursue practices above that of minimum regulatory compliance in order to continue to raise and retain assets. Turning to investors in particular, their enhanced operational due diligence efforts has caused them not only to become more informed about hedge fund compliance policies and procedures but also to demand enhanced compliance oversight and controls to ensure that funds are effectively managing compliance risks. This push has resulted in hedge funds striving for best practice compliance.

Distinguishing Best Practice Compliance from Industry Standards

When evaluating the quality of the compliance function in place at a hedge fund, investors often seek to compare the practices employed in one hedge fund to general industry practices. This is a process known as *benchmarking*. When approaching the benchmarking process, there are two common industry terms that are often utilized: industry standards and best practices.

Industry standard compliance, or *industry norm compliance*, refers to the compliance practices and procedures common in the hedge fund industry at a particular point in time. Some in the hedge fund industry utilize the terms *best practice compliance* and *industry norm compliance* interchangeably. This is presumably done on the assumption that, if the majority of the hedge funds are following a particular compliance practice, then it must be a best practice.

On the other hand, some investors draw a distinction between best practices and industry norms to better demonstrate the potential differences in place between the two standards. An example of how such distinctions might work is summarized in Exhibit 8.1.

To demonstrate how these terms are applied let us consider an example of the monitoring by the compliance function of employees' electronic communications. Today, it is considered a standard industry practice for some form of electronic communication monitoring to take place. This would be

Minimum Regulatory Compliance		Industry Standard Compliance		Best Practice Compliance
Complying with the minimum requirements of all laws and regulations applicable to the hedge fund to operate legally		Going beyond minimum regulatory compliance to institute compliance policies and procedures that are in-line with standard compliance practices in the hedge fund industry		Exceeding industry standard compliance and implementing compliance protocols adhering to industry best practices

EXHIBIT 8.1 Example of How Distinctions May Be Drawn between Different Levels of Hedge Fund Compliance

the industry standard. Said another way, if a hedge fund does not perform electronic communication monitoring, it is deviating from the common standards in place in the industry. To show how the terms "industry standard" and "best practice" may be used interchangeably, it is also a perfectly valid and true statement to say that it is best practice for a hedge fund to conduct electronic communication monitoring.

Now just because a hedge fund follows one element of best practices by monitoring its electronic communications that does not mean that is complying with all the best practices in that area. For example a hedge fund could drop below industry norms in the ways that electronic communications are monitored, who conducts the monitoring, and how frequently the monitoring is performed. Depending on the specific practices employed in these areas, a hedge fund may simply adhere to minimum requirements.

In practice, formalizing these distinctions when evaluating the compliance function can present several real-world problems for investors. The reasons for this include:

- *Lack of transparency on compliance practices*—The hedge fund industry is notoriously opaque, and the area of compliance is no exception. There is no publicly available database of global hedge fund compliance practices. This fosters an environment where it is not always immediately apparent in all areas of compliance what the specific industry norms are.
- *Diverse strategies and manager types*—Hedge funds are a diverse series of different fund manager types employing unique strategies. These differences do not easily facilitate an apples-to-apples comparison of compliance norms across hedge funds in all areas of compliance. For example, a fund that trades only equities may face much fewer compliance challenges in the area of valuation as compared to a distressed hedge fund that trades more illiquid positions.
- *Regional differences and accompanying different regulatory regimes*— There are regional differences reflected in the compliance programs

of different hedge funds. For example, a fund based in Hong Kong or Switzerland is subject to different series of minimum compliance requirements than a fund in the United States or the Cayman Islands. While there may be shared common elements of regulations across jurisdictions, there are enough material differences that comparisons of compliance practices on an individual country or regional basis can present challenges.

To cite a concrete example of the distinction between industry norm and best practices, we can consider a compliance practice referred to as a *mock audit*. This is when a hedge fund simulates an audit by a regulator. The primary purpose of this audit is to gauge preparedness for real regulatory examinations. Mock audits are discussed in more detail in Chapter 6.

Let us assume it is the industry norm for a hedge fund to undergo a mock audit at least once every five years. Next, consider a hedge fund that has never undergone a mock audit. That is a pretty straightforward scenario in which this fund deviates from industry norms. What about a hedge fund that has a mock audit performed every three years? They are certainly not only complying with the five-year industry norm but also exceeding it. Does this mean that they are in line with best practices? Not necessarily because while they are exceeding industry norms with regards to the frequency of the mock audits, other factors can go into evaluating mock audit best practices. The scope and depth of the mock audits is another element that would factor into the best practice analysis. If a hedge fund performs mock audits more frequently than the industry norm, but its mock audits are cursory in nature, when the industry standard would be to have more robust mock audits, then the fund would not be necessarily adhering to either industry standards or best practices. This example highlights some of the problems in drawing distinctions between classifying a certain approach as best practices form a compliance perspective.

Hedge funds are not ignorant of this fact either. Earlier we referenced the increased due diligence efforts paid by investors to operational areas, such as hedge fund compliance. Hedge funds understand that investors are increasingly interested in having their funds follow compliance best practices and may capitalize on the flexibility surrounding these terms, either intentionally or inadvertently, in response to investor due diligence inquiries and marketing efforts.

For example, a fund may tell a potential investor something to the effect of, *"We take compliance very seriously and seek to adhere to best practices, and that is why we perform mock audits on a three-year rolling cycle."* However, as we highlighted earlier in this discussion the frequency of mock audits may be only one determining factor in determining whether or not they are conducted on a best practices basis. As such, based on the hedge fund's description of the frequency of mock audits alone, it would be difficult for an investor to determine whether or not best practices were truly being employed. To help navigate this potential ambiguity in practice, regardless of whether one party refers to a compliance practice as industry norm or best practices, the important thing is the quality of the actual compliance policy or control that is in place.

KEY COMPLIANCE ANALYSIS AREAS

As investors go through the initial and ongoing compliance due diligence processes, they should endeavor to review all aspects of a hedge fund's compliance program. This includes an analysis of the role of the CCO, the resources of the compliance function in general, the adequacy of compliance training programs, the role of compliance committees, and the compliance oversight of electronic communications, cybersecurity, and business continuity and disaster recovery.

There are two additional related areas of increasing importance for investors as they seek to make evaluations of the strengths and weaknesses within compliance functions: (1) personal account dealing and (2) material nonpublic information.

Personal Account Dealing Analysis

Hedge funds make investments with money sourced from their clients. In addition, the employees of a hedge fund may wish to engage in personal securities transactions for their own personal trading accounts. This area of compliance is referred to as the area of *personal account dealing, personal trading,* or *personnel trading.* These personal account trades can be contrasted with trades that a hedge fund may execute on behalf of the funds it manages.

The types of accounts traditionally covered by these policies include employee accounts with brokerage capabilities and other discretionary accounts in which an employee has the power to make or influence investment decisions. The types of accounts typically not covered by these policies include:

- Savings plans and collective investment plans such as pension and retirement plans
- Mutual funds and unit investment trusts held directly at the fund distributor

- Dividend reinvestment plans
- Accounts without brokerage capability, including checking, savings, and money market accounts

Although employee trading is supposed to be completely separate from the trading activities of the hedge fund itself, there is a potential for conflicts to arise. Specifically, one of the primary conflicts is a practice known as *front running*. This refers to a practice in which an employee possesses advance knowledge that the hedge fund that they work for is going to be making a particular trade, and they benefit from this information by executing trades for their own personal account in advance.

To illustrate this, consider a hedge fund that is going to make a large purchase of shares of outstanding stock in a thinly traded company that would likely be significant enough to move the market higher for those shares. To benefit from this knowledge, the employee could rush out in advance of the fund and buy shares of the same stock for her own personal account. After the hedge fund proceeds with its trade, the stock price would likely significantly increase and the employee would benefit from her advance purchase of the stock. The problem with having employees front run the activities of the hedge fund is that it creates a disadvantage for the investors of the hedge fund in place of creating an advantage for the individual employee. As a result, many jurisdictions make the practice of front running illegal. A second potential area of conflict in regards to personal account dealing conflicts relates to the potential for trading in material nonpublic information (MNPI). This is also referred to as insider information, and conflicts related to MNPI are discussed in the next section.

To avoid even the appearance of any such conflicts, many hedge funds simply prohibit employees from trading for their own accounts. Even when such prohibitions are in place employees are generally allowed to make investments in retirement contributions accounts, which are passively managed by third parties.

When seeking to evaluate the compliance oversight of a hedge fund's personal account dealing policies and procedures some of the best practices investors can look for include the following personal account dealing oversight mechanisms:

- *Preclearance*: A hedge fund can require employees to have the vast majority of potential trades for their own personal account reviewed and approved by the compliance department prior to their execution. Those trades that would typically be exempted would be a select list of exceptions, such as retirement accounts, as noted above.

- An accompanying best practice in this area is to set a restriction on the time period for which preclearances are valid. The common wisdom in this area is that the shorter the window during which preclearance approvals are valid, the better. The reasoning for this thinking is that the investment activities of the hedge fund as well as the conditions of markets change frequently. Preclearances that are valid for a number of days may venture into territory where the potential for conflict may arise that could otherwise have been avoided if the validity of the preapproval window had been shortened. An example of a short preclearance approval window would be a policy that all preclearance approvals expire by the end of the trading day on which they are granted.
- *Postclearance*: This is a process by which the compliance department performs checks on the actual trades executed in an employee's personal brokerage account. The way these checks are performed is by collecting brokerage statements from employee accounts and comparing them to preclearance requests.

  The process by which these statements are collected represent an area of potential weakness in a hedge fund's compliance practices. It is considered best practice for the compliance department to collect copies of these brokerage statements directly from the brokers in order to preserve independence of the information.

  It is a weaker practice to have employees collect copies of brokerage statements from their personal brokers and then provide them to compliance. There is the potential for the employee to manipulate the information contained in the statements or to fabricate their own statements entirely, which they would not have the opportunity to do if they came directly from the broker to the compliance function. To facilitate the transfer of information, a number of hedge funds utilize systems that allow employees' personal account brokers to transmit the statements and trade details directly to the hedge fund electronically. Some hedge funds will only permit their employees to utilize brokers for their personal trading that have the ability to submit personal brokerage statements electronically.

  The goals of postclearance checks by compliance are twofold. First, postclearance checks allow the compliance function to ensure that preapproved trades were actually executed exactly as they were preapproved. For example, if the compliance function approved the purchase of 100 shares of a particular stock but the employee actually purchased 1,000 shares instead, this would be a violation of the original preapproval.

  Second, the goal of the postclearance process is to ensure that employees appropriately seek preapproval of all covered trades as required under the hedge fund's policies. When compliance collects a copy of a brokerage statement for postclearance review, it may show a trade executed by an employee in shares of IBM. The employee, however, may never have requested a preapproval from compliance to execute trades in IBM. This, therefore, would represent a violation of the compliance policies in this area.

- *Penalties for policy violation*: Technical violations of a hedge fund's personal account dealing policies can occur for a wide variety of reasons. As a deterrence, it is considered a best practice for a hedge fund to maintain some mechanisms to enforce penalties against employees that continually violate the policies. Violations can happen because an employee simply forgets to submit the preapproval. Such oversights do happen occasionally and are generally not cause for concern; however, if a particular employee regularly forgets to submit trades for preapproval, it should lead to disciplinary actions. Common penalties include requiring employees to disgorge any profits from violations and possibly include termination of employment in extreme circumstances.

- *Restricted lists*: To prevent potential conflicts between the trading activities of a hedge fund and its employees, often compliance departments will maintain a list of securities that employees are not permitted to invest in for their own personal accounts. To be clear, items on a restricted list are typically there on a temporary basis and are taken off of the list once a hedge fund's trading activities transition to obviate the specific conflicts surrounding the security having employees trade in the security. In some cases, compliance policies may be designed so as not to permit employees from transacting in any securities for their own brokerage accounts that are being held by the hedge fund. Another common prohibition is that employees cannot transact in any positions recently held by the hedge fund during a predetermined time period, such as within the last 60 days.

An example of how this would work in practice would be if a hedge fund took an active position in the stock of the General Electric Company (symbol: GE) and also 10 days ago sold out of a position in the Dow Chemical Company (symbol: DOW). If the hedge fund maintained personal trading prohibitions such as those described above, then both GE and DOW would be placed on the hedge fund's restricted list, and employees would not be permitted to transact in them until they were removed.

Historically, restricted lists were maintained in paper form by the compliance department and physically disseminated to employees. The preclearance process also served as a check to ensure that employees did not attempt to transact in securities placed on the restricted list.

Today, many hedge funds utilize software systems to assist in managing the personal account dealing process. This includes not only assisting with postclearance oversight but also managing preclearance and restricted list processes. In regard to restricted lists in particular, hedge funds may automatically load the securities that are not permitted to be traded by employees into the preclearance system. When an employee then attempts to submit a preclearance approval, the system would automatically notify them that the security is on the restricted list.

- *Minimum holding periods*: A minimum holding period is a predetermined minimum amount of time that an employee is required to hold purchases made in a personal brokerage account prior to selling out of them. One common exception to this rule is when an employee purchases a security for her personal brokerage account that significantly declines in value soon after the purchase is made. In these cases, hedge funds often permit employees to take advantage of a *hardship exemption* and sell out of the position. One reason this exemption is allowed is because personal account dealing policies are not intended to penalize employees that trade for their own account but rather to prevent potential conflicts of interest with the funds. When the employee takes a hardship exemption, there is little likelihood that the interest of the hedge fund's investors would be placed behind those of the employee.

A related compliance policy is the implementation of restrictions with regard to the volume of personal trades that may be conducted during any particular period. This policy, in conjunction with minimum holding periods, serves to promote a second goal of these types of minimum holding period policies, which is to discourage employees from focusing too actively on trading on behalf of their own account rather than on their primary jobs. An example of how these types of policies would work together would be if a hedge fund maintains a policy that states that employees are required to hold all positions for at least 60 days and are limited to no more than five trades in their personal accounts per month.

Material Nonpublic Information

In Chapter 2, we outlined how hedge fund regulators have increased their focus on analyzing the ways in which a hedge fund structures compliance rules and controls surrounding material nonpublic information (MNPI). In Chapter 4, we highlighted that compliance rules surrounding MNPI are a popular topic for specific compliance training sessions for hedge fund investment professionals. Investors too have increasingly focused on the ways in which hedge funds approach the compliance challenges surrounding MNPI.

When evaluating a hedge fund's compliance policies, an investor is likely to encounter language that outlines the ways in which MNPI is defined in the respective jurisdiction in which a hedge fund is based. To clarify further how the concept MNPI is commonly defined, what follows is an illustration of common MNPI policy language for a U.S.-based fund:

Material Information—Information is considered material if: (1) there is a substantial likelihood that a reasonable investor would consider it important in making his or her investment decisions; or (2) it would significantly alter the total mix of information made available.

Information is material if it has "market significance" in that the dissemination of such information is likely to affect the market price of the security (e.g., imminent block trade or revised research recommendation). For information to be considered material, it does not need to be important enough that it would have changed an investor's decision to purchase or sell particular securities, it would be enough that an investor would reasonably rely on making purchase or sale decisions.

Nonpublic Information—Nonpublic information is generally considered that type of information that has not been disseminated in a manner in which it is generally available to investors. An example of this would be when it is available through news services and investors have had a reasonable time to react to the information. Generally, there are two classifications of nonpublic information:

1. Issuer or corporate information, including details about future earnings and merger negotiations
2. Security demand and market information, such as pending trade order detail

Once the information has become public, it may generally be traded on freely.

One of the reasons investors are increasingly concerned about MNPI is due to enhanced enforcement actions by regulators for violations in this area. A common description of U.S. penalties outlined in hedge fund compliance materials for MNPI violations follows.

An individual may be subjected to penalties even if he does not personally benefit from communicating or trading on material nonpublic information. Penalties in this area can include:

1. A permanent bar from association with firms, including brokers, dealers, investment, or investment advisers
2. Disgorgement of profits
3. Civil injunctions
4. With regard to the person that committed the violation, civil penalties of up to three times the profit gained or loss avoided
5. For the employer or other controlling person of the person that performed the violation, civil penalties that could go up to three times the amount of the profit gained or loss avoided as a result of each violation
6. Criminal penalties including the potential for large fines and extensive jail time

Expert Networks Over the past few years, the avenues by which hedge funds may become exposed to MNPI through the investment research process have increased. One of the drivers has been the growth of the expert network industry. *Expert networks* are companies that provide a matchmaking service between specific individuals and hedge funds. These individuals are referred to as experts because they typically have particular experience in different industries that may be useful for hedge funds in considering potential investment opportunities. For example, a hedge fund may consider making an investment in a company that manufactures semiconductors but may not be familiar with recent trends in the industry. Speaking to a recently retired executive from that industry would likely provide useful insights to the hedge fund.

Although the experts the hedge funds speaks to are not supposed to provide MNPI, the risks for transmission, either intentionally or inadvertently, are present. Investors seeking to evaluate a hedge fund's potential compliance liabilities as it relates to MNPI, therefore, are increasingly focusing on the way hedge funds interact with expert networks. In evaluating a hedge fund's compliance oversight of expert networks, important factors investors can evaluate would be whether the hedge fund employs the following best practices in this area:

- *The hedge fund performs due diligence on the expert network*: It is important for hedge funds to perform due diligence on the ways in which an expert network seeks to prevent the transmission of MNPI from its experts to a hedge fund. Investors should evaluate how thoroughly a hedge fund has evaluated the expert network, including understanding the compliance framework in place at the expert network, as well as the training and vetting processes for experts.

- *The hedge fund communicates its own compliance policies to the expert network*: In addition to MNPI controls that may be in place at the expert network, it is also important for hedge funds to proactively give the expert network the hedge fund's own MNPI-related compliance policies. The reason for this is there may be differences in place between the hedge funds own policies and the expert network. In many cases, hedge funds have stricter prohibitions in place than the expert network may have. In these cases, if the hedge fund is to utilize the expert network, special measures should be taken to ensure that the hedge fund's policies are complied with. An example of how a hedge fund may bridge this gap in practice is by having a hedge fund employee read a disclaimer prior to speaking to an expert that is prepared by the hedge fund's compliance department. This disclaimer would reiterate the specific policies of the hedge fund in this area and highlight that the employee does not wish to receive MNPI from the expert.

- *Preclearance of experts*: Prior to having a hedge fund's employees engage in any discussion with experts, it is considered best practice to have them preclear the use of specific experts through a hedge fund's compliance departments rather than working directly with the expert network. The purpose of this is to allow the compliance function to vet the use of any potential experts while keeping in mind any potential conflicts that may be in place as it relates to current or planned investments of the firm's funds.

- *Limitations on expert public company experience*: If an expert currently works or has recently worked for a publicly traded company, many hedge funds seek to maintain enhanced restrictions on any conversations a hedge fund's employees may have with this expert. If the hedge fund were to make trades related to the public company, where the expert has recent direct experience, there is an enhanced risk that MNPI could be discussed that the hedge fund may then act upon.

    Some hedge funds maintain policies that explicitly prohibit their employees from speaking to experts currently working at public companies. In addition, hedge fund policies may also not allow employees to speak to experts who have worked at a public company within a predetermined time period, such as the last 12 months.

- *Compliance auditing of expert calls*: It is best practice for a hedge fund's compliance function to maintain a mechanism for auditing the actual calls between the hedge fund employee and the expert. The most common mechanisms utilized is for a representative of compliance to actually listen into the calls in conjunction with the hedge fund employee as they speak to the expert. While it is ideal for compliance to listen in to every call in some cases, depending on the resources in place at the hedge fund, compliance may instead opt to randomly select the calls to audit or only listen to a portion of all calls.
- *Preparation of expert call summaries*: It is best practice for the employees of the hedge fund that spoke to the expert to prepare a summary memorandum of the expert call. These summaries serve to develop a written log of which experts were spoken to on which dates. In addition, these summaries also create documentation of the topics and specific companies discussed during the call. These summaries facilitate the monitoring and testing of expert activity, as well as allowing the hedge fund to provide documentation to regulators in the event that questions arise relating to a hedge fund potentially trading in MNPI.
- *Monitoring and testing of expert requests and conversations*: As noted above, it is best practice for the compliance function to monitor the use of experts by employees. As part of this monitoring, the compliance function should note whether a hedge fund employee, such as an investment analyst, consistently talks to the same expert. With frequent usage of the same expert, there is an enhanced potential for the analyst to push too far in asking for information about a particular subject, which could venture into the realm of MNPI.

In addition, it is best practice for the compliance department to monitor the specific companies discussed during expert calls to determine whether a hedge fund is actively using this information in violation of MNPI rules. This can be the case even if multiple different experts are utilized. For example, if over the course of a month, a hedge fund's investment analyst talks to 15 different experts about the prospects of a particular company and then the hedge fund actively trades in that company over the same period, these trades should be subjected to a higher degree of scrutiny by the compliance department to determine whether MNPI was a factor in executing those trades. This would include reviewing the content of the conversation between the analyst and the experts, evaluating the timing and specifics of the hedge fund's trades, as well as the specific items discussed with the experts in order to determine whether any potential violations took place.

CHAPTER SUMMARY

This chapter highlighted the process by which investors evaluate a hedge fund's compliance function. Our discussion began with an introduction to the concepts of investment and operational due diligence processes. We next discussed how a review of a hedge fund's compliance function, policies, and procedures are integrated into the initial and ongoing compliance process. This discussion included an overview of the three key stages in the initial compliance analysis process. We then turned our discussion toward how investors seek to evaluate a hedge fund's culture of compliance as well as compliance best practices. Finally, we highlighted hedge fund best practices in two key related compliance areas that are increasingly analyzed by investors: (1) employee personal account dealing and (2) compliance policies regarding MNPI.

Now that we have introduced the ways in which investors analyze compliance functions, in the next chapter we will continue to focus on the practical applications of compliance through analysis of example scenarios and case studies.

NOTE

1. For reference, the 2015–2016 business plans are available at www.fca.org.uk/static/channel-page/business-plan/business-plan-2015-16.html.

CHAPTER 9

Case Studies and Example Scenarios in Hedge Fund Compliance

INTRODUCTION

To demonstrate some of the common challenges facing the practical application of daily hedge fund compliance, this chapter begins by providing illustrative hypothetical compliance scenarios. At the end of each scenario, a series of concept questions are featured to further help frame the discussion. We then provide a summary of historical case scenarios that illustrate key topics in compliance.

COMPLIANCE SCENARIO 1

In this scenario, we present a discussion between a Chief Compliance Officer (CCO), Mr. A, who is being interviewed by a prospective investor during the due diligence process. In reviewing this scenario, see what cues you can pick up on regarding the strengths and weaknesses of the hedge fund's compliance program, with a particular focus on the knowledge of the CCO regarding the firm's compliance policies.

Prospective Investor: Thank you for meeting with me, Mr. A. As you know, I am here on behalf of my organization to perform due diligence on your hedge fund regarding a potential investment. As part of this process, I am looking to evaluate the compliance function in place at your firm. Can you provide me with a summary of it?

Mr. A: Yes, as CCO my job is to run the compliance function. I joined the firm three years ago from a big bank. Once I was in place as CCO here, we worked with a law firm to assist us in reviewing all of our offering documentation.

Prospective Investor: Did the law firm help with any of the compliance documentation as well, such as the compliance manual or code of ethics?

Mr. A: Based on my experience and previous compliance materials I had used at the bank, I took the lead on drafting those, but the law firm reviewed them.

Prospective Investor: Is the compliance function just yourself?

Mr. A: Well, I run it with assistance from Ms. B, who is a shared employee who also helps the fund accounting and operations groups.

Prospective Investor: Can you describe the different compliance duties performed by Ms. B and yourself?

Mr. A: On an annual basis, Ms. B makes sure every employee signs an attestation to ensure that they have read and complied with our firm's compliance policies and procedures. She also collects and reviews personal trading account statements. Our law firm makes sure we comply with annual training requirements, and I oversee the whole process.

Prospective Investor: Understood. Are there any backup personnel for Ms. B?

Mr. A: No, but we feel based on the size of our firm our staffing is appropriate.

Prospective Investor: What about things like monitoring electronic communications?

Mr. A: We have those archived so Ms. B can review them if we need to, but we don't actively police them—our employees know our policies in this regard.

Prospective Investor: As far as your role goes, that doesn't sound like a full-time job for you. Do you have any other responsibilities?

Mr. A: Yes. I am also the Chief Financial Officer, Chief Operating Officer, and President of the firm.

Prospective Investor: With so many titles, do you feel you have adequate time to focus on the compliance function?

Mr. A: Yes, and don't forget that I have Ms. B to support me. I also occasionally reach out to our law firm with questions.

Prospective Investor: That makes sense. Can you tell me what you do with regard to employee training?

Mr. A: As required by our regulator, we conduct compliance training for all employees once each year. Also, as I mentioned, each employee must attest they have read and complied with our compliance policies each year.

Prospective Investor: What changes have you made to the compliance program over the past three years to comply with new regulatory guidelines?

Mr. A: Our compliance program is pretty plain vanilla. We don't trade anything complicated for our funds, so there hasn't been much need for change. We also rely on our investors to provide us with feedback if they feel there is something we need to be doing better.

Prospective Investor: When was the last time you were audited by a financial regulator?

Mr. A: We were visited once approximately five years ago before I joined, and we haven't been visited since.

Prospective Investor: Have you ever considered having a third-party mock audit performed?

Mr. A: That would take up too much of my time. Remember, I also have to focus on my other duties as COO, CFO, and President. Besides, I feel we are prepared for a regulatory audit. Everything we do is straightforward.

Prospective Investor: With you being focused on your other duties, would it be fair to say that Ms. B does most of the day-to-day compliance work?

Mr. A: Yes, subject to my oversight.

Prospective Investor: Does she or you have any training in compliance?

Mr. A: No. No specific training, but we both have many years' experience and have never had any issues. We have a strong culture of compliance here.

Concept Questions

1. How would you evaluate the quality of the overall compliance function?
2. Based on this conversation, what are its strengths and weaknesses?
3. What other questions would you ask the CCO, Mr. A, in order to evaluate the compliance function?
4. What is your opinion regarding Mr. A's statement that he developed the hedge fund's compliance documentation based on his knowledge of the bank's compliance materials?
5. Would your answer change if we assumed the hedge fund and the division of the bank he worked for maintained similar investment strategies?
6. Do you feel Mr. A and Ms. B are qualified to run the compliance program? If not, how would you correct this?
7. What steps could the hedge fund take to enhance its compliance function?
8. Do you feel the use of the law firm by the hedge fund was appropriate in this case? What could have been done to improve upon the effectiveness of the use of third parties in assisting the compliance function?

Summary

Although it may be easy to simply dismiss this hedge fund's compliance function as being poorly managed based on Mr. A's shared responsibilities and lack of dedicated oversight, investors may indeed encounter such situations when they evaluate compliance functions in the real world. The question facing many investors, all other things being equal, is whether a weak compliance function would represent a significant enough risk to prevent investment.

From the perspective of the hedge fund, there may be a number of items based on the scope of their business they feel are handled appropriately. For example, when Mr. A joined the firm, he engaged a third-party law firm to assist in reviewing certain documentation. The problem becomes, however, that we do not have enough detail on what the scope of the law firm's review was. For example, did they conduct an actual audit of the hedge fund's compliance practices and compare them to the description of practices in the compliance manual? Furthermore, the timing of the law firm's review of documentation raises questions. Why were no more frequent ongoing reviews of documentation conducted?

In addition, based on Mr. A's description, the hedge fund manages a fairly straightforward compliance function and may not have too much compliance work on a day-to-day basis. Assuming that this is indeed the case, a lack of day-to-day compliance work would not remove the need for ongoing evaluations of the hedge fund's larger compliance framework in areas, including compliance testing, personal account dealing oversight, and cybersecurity. The fact that training is only conducted annually and the firm has never undergone a mock audit also presents areas for concern. In summary, more information is needed to fully evaluate this compliance function; however, when a CCO shares too many different roles and is similarly supported by shared staff, coupled with the fact that there is no support from a compliance consultant, weaknesses such as these develop in the compliance function.

COMPLIANCE SCENARIO 2

In this scenario, we will present a section of a discussion between a CCO, Mr. B, and an existing investor during ongoing monitoring of the compliance function. When reading this discussion, consider the authoritative nature by which the CCO attempts to answer the questions posed.

Existing Investor: Now let's turn to the area of outside business activities.

    Mr. B: Yes. We have detailed policies in this area contained in our compliance manual.

    Existing Investor: Yes, I have reviewed the policies, but can you please summarize them again for me?

    Mr. B: Of course. While permitted in limited instances, we discourage employees from participating in outside business activities. Therefore, the majority of our employees don't do this. Also any such activities require preclearance from compliance.

    Existing Investor: How is this preclearance documented?

    Mr. B: Through e-mail, but as I said, it rarely happens.

    Existing Investor: Have you not allowed anyone to participate in outside activities they have requested approval for?

    Mr. B: No. Most people understand the policy and that we discourage those activities, so they don't actively pursue them.

    Existing Investor: Does anyone currently have any outside business activities that you are aware of?

    Mr. B: Our Chief Investment Officer sits on the board of his alma mater but that is it.

    Existing Investor: Are you sure? Would you like to double check your records?

    Mr. B: No, I'm positive that's it. Remember, as CCO I am required to approve all of these activities.

    Existing Investor: I see. Well prior to our meeting we performed some background searches and noticed that several employees of the hedge fund sit on the boards of companies. Why did you omit these in your previous answer?

    Mr. B: Um, I am not sure ...

Concept Questions

1. Do you feel Mr. B was actively lying to the existing investor? Or instead was he simply ignorant of these other outside business activities?
2. What message does this send about the culture of compliance in the firm?

3. Do you think that Mr. B was too reliant on his employees to oversee themselves in this area?
4. Do you feel that Mr. B's responses merit concerns for the rest of the compliance program?
5. a. Do you think Mr. B's ignorance of these other outside business activities would have come up if the investor had simply taken his word at face value instead of doing checks prior to the interview?
   b. If not, what implication does this have if instead a financial regulator had asked these questions instead of an existing investor? Would the potential consequences have been different?
6. What corrective action would you suggest this fund take?

Scenario 2 Summary

This scenario demonstrates the importance of being prepared as an investor prior to conducting a due diligence meeting focused on the compliance function. It is particularly easy for an existing investor to assume that since their prior due diligence might not have raised any red flags, the compliance function is continuing to operate smoothly. As this example demonstrates, this may not always be the situation. In this case, there are two scenarios: Either Mr. B is either actively lying to perhaps demonstrate that the employees of the fund are not distracted with other outside business activities or there is simply weak compliance oversight in this area. Giving him the benefit of the doubt, the more likely scenario is the latter.

Perhaps the problem is that employees have not been appropriately trained and do not submit the e-mail requests to Mr. B for preapproval. Another point to note is that Mr. B should have not so definitively answered the question simply to keep the meeting moving forward, but instead taken the opportunity afforded to him by the investor to check on this issue and then follow up with the investor. If indeed he had made this statement to a regulator, Mr. B and the hedge fund may have been in more serious trouble rather than simply potentially losing the investment of this existing investor.

CASE STUDIES

Scenarios are useful for demonstrating hypothetical situations that hedge fund compliance professionals and investors may find themselves in. Case studies are illustrative of actual real-world compliance challenges hedge funds have already faced. By highlighting the compliance failures of firms in different situations, we can learn how to avoid these situations and pursue best practices. In this section, we will include summaries which demonstrate compliance challenges faced by hedge funds and as well as key concept questions to consider in each circumstance.

Case Study 1:

The matter of John Thomas Capital Management Group LLC, et al., is a case that dates back from 2013. In this case, the U.S. Securities and Exchange Commission (SEC) charged a Houston-based hedge fund manager and his firm of defrauding investors in two hedge funds and steering inflated fees to a brokerage firm CEO who was also charged in the SEC's case.[1]

What follows is an excerpt of the allegations as outlined in the SEC's March 22, 2013, news digest.[2] In reviewing these allegations, keep in mind the relevant best practice compliance principles discussed up to this point in the book. As an exercise, see whether you can put together a bulleted list of the key alleged violations as well as what corrective action you would have recommended to the fund if you had been the CCO?

> "An investigation by the SEC's Enforcement Division found that George R. Jarkesy Jr., worked closely with Thomas Belesis to launch two hedge funds that raised $30 million from investors. Jarkesy and his firm John Thomas Capital Management (since renamed Patriot28 LLC) inflated valuations of the funds' assets, causing the value of investors' shares to be overstated and his management and incentive fees to be increased. Jarkesy, a frequent media commentator and radio talk show host, also lied to investors about the identity of the funds' auditor and prime broker.
>
> "Meanwhile, although they shared the same 'John Thomas' brand name, Jarkesy's firm and Belesis's firm, John Thomas Financial, were portrayed as wholly independent. Jarkesy led investors to believe that as manager of the funds, he was solely responsible for all investment decisions. However, Belesis sometimes supplanted Jarkesy as the decision maker and directed some investments from the hedge funds into a company in which his firm was heavily invested. Belesis also bullied Jarkesy into showering excessive fees on John Thomas Financial even in instances where the firm had done virtually nothing to earn them.
>
> "'Jarkesy disregarded the basic standards to which all fund managers are held,' said Andrew M. Calamari, Director of the SEC's New York Regional Office. 'Not only did he falsify valuations and deceive investors about the value of their holdings, but he bent over backwards

to enrich Belesis at the funds' expense. Belesis in turn exploited the supposed independence of the funds to surreptitiously pull the strings on key decisions.'

"According to the SEC's order instituting administrative proceedings against Jarkesy, Belesis, and their firms, Jarkesy launched the two hedge funds in 2007 and 2009, and they were called John Thomas Bridge and Opportunity Fund LP I and John Thomas Bridge and Opportunity Fund LP II. The funds invested in three asset classes: bridge loans to start-up companies, equity investments principally in microcap companies, and life settlement policies. Jarkesy mispriced certain holdings to increase the net asset values of the funds, which were the basis for calculating the management and incentive fees that Jarkesy deducted from the funds for himself. Jarkesy also falsely claimed that prominent service providers such as KPMG and Deutsche Bank worked with the funds.

"According to the SEC's order, Jarkesy used fund assets to hire multiple stock promoters in 2010 and 2011 to create an artificial and unsustainable spike in the price of two microcap stocks in which the funds were heavily invested. As a result of these efforts, the funds recorded temporary gains in the value of the microcap stocks that Jarkesy used to mask the write-down of other more illiquid holdings of the funds.

"According to the SEC's order, Jarkesy violated his fiduciary duties to the funds in multiple instances by providing excessive compensation to Belesis and John Thomas Financial. This only incited further demands by Belesis. For example, in February 2009, Belesis angrily complained via e-mail that Jarkesy was not steering enough money to John Thomas Financial, and Jarkesy responded that 'we will always try to get you as much as possible, Everytime [*sic*] without exception!' On another occasion, Jarkesy reassured Belesis that '[n]obody gets access to Tommy until they make us money!!!!!'

"The SEC's order charges that Jarkesy and John Thomas Capital Management violated and aided and abetted violations of Section 17(a) of the Securities Act and Section 10(b) of the Securities Exchange Act and Rule 10b-5, and violated Sections 206(1), 206(2), and 206(4) of the Investment Advisers Act and Rule 206(4)-8. The SEC's order further charges that Belesis and John Thomas Financial aided and abetted and caused Jarkesy's and John Thomas Capital Management's violations of Sections 206(1), 206(2), and 206(4) of the Advisers Act and Rule 206(4)-8."

This case study is but one example of charges brought around the same time by the U.S. SEC against hedge funds that included allegations of inflated valuations. Examples of other cases include:

- *SEC v. RKC Capital Mgmt.*, LLC, No. 12-cv-408 (D. Utah Apr. 30, 2012)
- *SEC v. Yorkville Advisors*, LLC, No. 12-cv-7728 (S.D.N.Y. Oct. 17, 2012)

Case Study 1 Concept Questions

1. One of the SEC's allegations related to inflated valuations of assets:
   a. Do you think it is likely that effective valuation committee was maintained in this case?
   b. If not, why do you think that this was so from a compliance perspective?
   c. What documentation do you think any valuation committees that were in place should have prepared?
   d. What role, if any, would a CCO have played in ensuring that the valuations were appropriate?

2. On a related note, the SEC alleged that the inflated valuations caused excessive fees to be generated.
   a. What role can a CCO play in overseeing that the fees charged are appropriate?
   b. Do you feel the CCO should take the lead on this matter or is it better left for other individuals such as the CFO or perhaps even fund service providers that are more involved in fee calculations such as the fund administrator or auditor?

3. Another allegation by the SEC was that relationships with certain service providers were claimed that did not actually exist.
   a. What role, if any, can compliance play in ensuring that fraudulent claims are not made to investors?
   b. Do you think that a hedge fund's legal function can play a role in this as well?

4. One of the allegations raised by the SEC related to the issue of which individuals investors may have believed were making investment decisions at the fund, as compared to who the actual decision makers may have been. Part of the role of a hedge fund compliance function is to ensure that the fund is operated in compliance with its core operating documentation. This documentation typically includes a description of who has investment making decision authority. What steps do you feel a hedge fund's compliance function could take to ensure investment decision-making authority is properly executed?

5. Another allegation raised by the SEC related to the alleged hiring of stock promoters to create spikes in the prices of two microcap stock in which the funds were invested.
   a. If you were this hedge fund's CCO, would you have permitted the alleged hiring of stock promoters? Why or why not?
   b. What role do you feel compliance should play in vetting the use of any third-party service providers such as the stock promoters that were referenced in these allegations?
   c. How should compliance conduct ongoing monitoring of these relationships?

Case Study 1 Summary There is a risk that a hedge fund's compliance function may focus too heavily on more traditional areas of compliance policies and procedures and not become involved enough in other areas such as evaluating the reasonableness valuations and fees. These risks are particularly highlighted in smaller hedge funds where compliance personnel often share multiple responsibilities, and may not leverage enough or at all on the use of third-party resources, such as compliance consultants, to augment their compliance functions. Cases such as these highlight the need for compliance to be an integral part of a hedge fund's ongoing operations.

Case Study 2

In 2013, the SEC began an initiative regarding the enforcement of violations relating to SEC Rule 105 of Regulation M. This rule is primarily concerned with short selling that could artificially depress market prices.[3] Without delving too deeply into all of its technicalities, a primary goal of the rule is designed to prevent a practice whereby a fund manager would benefit from purchasing securities in what are known as follow-on and secondary offerings, while at the same time the fund manager has entered into short-sale transactions in those securities prior to the pricing of the offering. The rule outlines that the prohibition on short sales typically extends for a restricted period that is generally five business days before the public offering. There are also special situations in which specific exceptions to the rule exist.

As part of this Rule 105 initiative, in 2013 the SEC announced that it was charging 23 firms with short-selling violations, including several hedge funds.[4] Although such violations may seem to be only minor technical violations, they can have material financial consequences for funds. At the time, 22 of the firms charged settled the enforcement actions, resulting in more than $14.4 million in sanctions. These fines typically involve the disgorgement of profits earned under the violation, as well as prejudgment interest and penalties. To give you an example of how these fines break down, some of the settlements paid in this situation include:[5]

- War Chest Capital Partners agreed to pay disgorgement of $187,036.17, prejudgment interest of $10,533.18, and a penalty of $130,000.00.
- Southpoint Capital Advisors agreed to pay disgorgement of $346,568.00, prejudgment interest of $17,695.76, and a penalty of $170,494.00.
- Talkot Capital agreed to pay disgorgement of $17,640.00, prejudgment interest of $1,897.68, and a penalty of $65,000.00.
- Merus Capital Partners agreed to pay disgorgement of $8,402.00, prejudgment interest of $63.65, and a penalty of $65,000.00.

In general, there are also typically large legal fees incurred by hedge funds in negotiating settlements with the SEC. In this case, the SEC also required certain firms to refrain from participating in secondary and follow-on offerings for one year.[6] In addition, the SEC required firms to certify, in writing, compliance with the rule, including providing written evidence of compliance in the form of a narrative, supported by exhibits. Interestingly, the rule applies regardless of whether the purchaser intended to be manipulative, and the SEC has seemingly taken a zero-tolerance policy to violations in this regard.[7]

For these types of Rule 105 violations, the SEC previously noted that the reasons for historical Rule 105 violations in other cases had included:[8]

- Investment personnel either misunderstood or were unaware of the rule's requirements
- The firm's compliance manual did not address it
- The firm lacked policies and procedures sufficient to prevent the violations

Case Study 2: Concept Questions

1. What measures do you think these hedge funds could have taken to prevent the violations of Rule 105 of Regulation M?
2. Do you feel that compliance-related-trading technology could have played a part in preventing these violations? If so, how?
3. An element highlighted by the SEC for historical rule violations included misunderstandings of the rule or a complete lack of awareness of it. As CCO of a hedge fund, what would you have done to particularly address that point?
4. Another historical contributing factor to rule violations highlighted by the SEC was that the firm's compliance documentation and policies did not adequately address the rule.
   a. Assuming that some of the hedge funds that violated the rule had dedicated compliance personnel, utilized compliance consultants, and had well-defined relationships with legal counsel, how could such violations occur?
   b. What lessons can be learned from this about the frequency of compliance documentation updates?

Case Study 2 Summary With the volume and complexity of hedge fund regulations increasing, the full ramifications of sometimes seemingly minor technical rule changes may be overlooked. In addition, financial regulators may change their enforcement priorities and suddenly start to focus more heavily on enforcing practices previously not heavily regulated. As the Rule 105 of Regulation M actions demonstrate, ongoing vigilance is required by a hedge fund's compliance department to ensure that policies and procedures are frequently updated to reflect revised rule changes. Even if the compliance policies are up to date with the most recent legislation and regulatory rules, the obligation is still on the hedge fund's compliance department to ensure the firm's employees are both aware of the rules and actively trained on them.

As the number of opportunities for technical violations of rules continues to increase, the compliance function should ensure that appropriate resources on in place, including leveraging on technology to assist in overseeing potential trade violations. In the case of this rule, technology could be used to code fund level trading restrictions into the firm's trading systems to attempt to automatically alert the compliance department, as well as investment personnel, of any potential violations before they occur. The oversight of the types of technical rules cannot be entirely outsourced to technology and should still be overseen by the manual human oversight of compliance personnel as well.

CHAPTER SUMMARY

Two hypothetical compliance scenarios featuring discussions between investors and CCOs were highlighted. In each case, there were deficiencies in the compliance programs noted. While it is tempting to focus solely on these deficiencies, the purpose of these scenarios is to highlight not only what may be wrong with a particular compliance function but also how issues can be corrected. We next proceeded to evaluate two case studies in which the SEC alleged compliance failings in hedge funds on a variety of issues, including inflated valuations, conflicts of interest, and violations of specific regulations. These cases demonstrate the real-world challenges of planning and management of an effective compliance function.

In the next chapter, we will continue to develop our understanding of the real-world application of hedge fund compliance principles by discussing common pitfalls that hedge funds may face in managing their compliance functions.

NOTES

1. The full name of the case is the matter of John Thomas Capital Management Group LLC d/b/a Patriot28 LLC and George R. Jarkesy, Jr.

2. U.S. Securities and Exchange Commission, "SEC Charges Hedge Fund Manager and Brokerage CEO with Fraud," *SEC News Digest*, no. 2013-55 (March 22, 2013), www.sec.gov/news/digest/2013/dig032213.htm.
3. National Exam Program Risk Alert, "Rule 105 of Regulation M: Short Selling in Connection with a Public Offering," vol. 3, no. 4 (September 17, 2013).
4. U.S. Securities and Exchange Commission, "SEC Charges 23 Firms with Short Selling Violations in Crackdown on Potential Manipulation in Advance of Stock Offerings," press release, September 2013.
5. Ibid.
6. See "In the Matter of War Chest Capital Partners LLC," release no. 34-76140, October 14, 2015.
7. See "In re Genesis Advisory Services Corp., ABJ Societe Anonyme Corp., and Bruce J. Fixelle," release no. 34-72212, May 21, 2014.
8. See Carlson Capital L.P., Exchange Act release no. 62982, September 23, 2010.

CHAPTER 10

Common Compliance Pitfalls and How to Avoid Them

INTRODUCTION

There are a number of real-world challenges toward implementing and managing a successful hedge fund compliance program. In this chapter, we will highlight six common compliance pitfalls and provide advice on how they can be avoided.

Please keep in mind that this list of pitfalls is by no means comprehensive. Each hedge fund is unique and will present its own series of potential compliance challenges; however, keeping these common mistakes in mind can assist you in minimizing the opportunity for mistakes, while capitalizing on the strengths of each particular organization.

PITFALL 1: SMALL FIRMS BUILD LARGE FIRM COMPLIANCE INFRASTRUCTURES

If you were to launch a new hedge fund today, from a compliance perspective you might feel that the hedge fund industry had already set the bar fairly high. This would be particularly true if you were to launch a smaller fund, let's say $25 million in total assets under management, with four full-time employees. Let us also assume that you utilized a reputable law firm to help you register with the relevant regulators and to prepare your compliance manual, but your Chief Compliance Officer (CCO), based on the size of your firm, understandably also has a number of other responsibilities.

Investors that were approaching your hedge fund would likely also be investors in other much larger hedge funds. Those larger funds would also most likely have large, well-established compliance functions, consisting of teams of dedicated compliance professionals. These larger funds might also have extensively utilized the service of third-party compliance consultants and law firms for services, including mock audits, cybersecurity plan development, and compliance training. How is a smaller hedge fund supposed to impress investors and compete against these larger, better-resourced funds?

From a compliance perspective, the infrastructures of smaller and larger hedge funds are not necessarily supposed to be equal in all areas. A common risk many newly launched or smaller hedge fund managers face, however, is that they feel pressured into overdelivering in the area of compliance. This results in a situation in which a smaller firm develops a compliance function that is better geared towards a much larger firm. An example would be a hedge fund manager that develops its compliance policies and procedures utilizing boilerplate documentation that was created with a much larger hedge fund in mind. This can create two primary problems.

The first is that the hedge fund's compliance policies and procedures will not describe the practices actually employed at the fund. This results in a widening of the policy/practice gap, a concept introduced in Chapter 7. Regulators increasingly focus on these disconnects and may sanction and fine hedge funds whose compliance policies describe practices that differ from those actually employed at the funds.

The second primary problem is that it is often too difficult for the smaller hedge funds to continually adhere to policies more appropriate for larger funds. Even if a small hedge fund starts off with good intentions of following myriad robust policies that may be more appropriate for larger funds, the funds do not often have the compliance resources to continue implementing these policies in a timely manner. For example, a smaller hedge fund may attempt to conduct extensive monitoring of employee electronic communications, say, to review 30 percent of all e-mails every month. However, in the same small fund, the CCO may perform several other roles and not have day-to-day compliance support. For the first few months of this policy, the CCO may indeed adhere to this 30 percent guideline but invariably other priorities will arise and they will not be able to keep up. This will result in a violation of their compliance policies and they would have instead been better off setting a more reasonable goal-based policy on the perceived compliance risks and resources of the firm.

The compliance function of a $25 million hedge fund is markedly different from a $1 billion fund. The larger hedge fund simply has more compliance work to be done. Most investors in particular, when considering an investment in a smaller hedge fund, understand these differences and that it would not be a fair apples-to-apples comparison in all areas between the two compliance functions at a small versus large firm. This is not to say that the smaller hedge fund should be given an excuse to cut corners on compliance, but rather that the compliance function of a smaller fund should be designed to be appropriate for the organization.

PITFALL 2: UNDERSPENDING ON COMPLIANCE

Hedge funds may sometimes seek to cut corners in their compliance programs and under spend on compliance. This underspending can occur in both smaller and larger hedge funds.

A common example of underspending in larger hedge funds would be in compliance training. As hedge funds continue to raise assets from investors over time, they transition from being smaller to larger firms. In some cases, depending on factors, including the capacity of the particular hedge fund strategy and the demand from investors, this growth may occur quite quickly, with a hedge fund raising hundreds of millions of dollars in a particular year. With such rapid growth typically comes a host of new hires in multiple departments to facilitate putting this new capital to work and the supporting infrastructure that it requires. When these new hires are made, the resources of the compliance function become increasingly strained in areas such as training. Particularly when individuals are joining the firm in multiple roles, and perhaps in multiple offices, compliance may develop a lag in the speed in which new hire compliance training is conducted. In addition, because of the increased demand for limited compliance resources, ongoing training, outside of regulatory required minimum sessions, may not occur as frequently.

The solution, of course, is to add commensurate compliance resources alongside the other new hires. However, when the focus of senior management is placed too heavily on the investment side of their businesses, compliance is one of the areas that may lag behind in terms of resources and policy revisions.

In smaller hedge funds, a common area in which underspending on compliance may occur is in cybersecurity, with a particular focus on penetration testing. *Penetration testing* refers to the practice of simulating unauthorized entry into a hedge fund's computer systems. In recent years, the definition has expanded to include items such as *social engineering hacking*, which is when a hacker attempts to trick not a computer system, but a human being into revealing information through information gained about that individual via methods such as social networks and other web searches. Another type of penetration testing refers to testing the physical security in place at a hedge fund. The areas of cybersecurity and penetration testing runs the risk of underspending because, until these types of attacks actually happen, it is easy for firms to place resources in other areas that have a more up-front presence in the day-to-day activities of the firm such as on enhanced business development efforts. In practice, however, many hedge funds undergo daily attacks from hackers seeking to infiltrate the firm's systems.

Regardless of a hedge funds size, the risks to funds from these types of attacks is quite real and has increased in recent years. One technique used by fraudsters to target hedge funds through social engineering hacking is a so-called Friday afternoon scam. This scam was utilized against a London hedge fund in 2013. An individual telephoned Fortelus Capital Management LLP's Chief Financial Officer Thomas Meston on a Friday afternoon. He claimed to be from the online fraud response team of Coutts, the hedge fund's bank that is a unit of Royal Bank of Scotland Group Plc.[1] The individual, who identified himself as Simon Hughes, claimed that there may have been fraudulent activity on the hedge fund's account and requested that the CFO generate codes for Mr. Hughes to cancel 15 suspicious payments.[2] The fraudster utilized the codes to steal £742,668, approximately $1.2 million, from the firm's accounts.[3] Mr. Meston was terminated and was sued by Fortelus alleging he breached his duty to protect the firm's assets.[4]

PITFALL 3: LACK OF INDEPENDENT COMPLIANCE REPORTING

Another common flaw hedge fund compliance functions may overlook relates to the reporting structure of the compliance function itself. Within the organization, the reporting line of the CCO may not be independently structured. In these cases, the CCO may have additional layers of personnel in place above her. This can be referred to as an *indirect compliance reporting structure*. It can create potential conflicts of interest and preclude the CCO from independently reporting compliance risks directly to the firm's senior management. The risks are common in both larger hedge funds, which have more levels of fund reporting, as well as smaller funds in which the CCO role may be shared and reporting lines may be blurred.

An example would be if the CCO reports first to a Chief Operating Officer who then reports to the firm's senior management. This presents a potentially dangerous situation whereby certain compliance risks may be underreporting or minimized by those individuals in-between the CCO and senior management. Regulators have acknowledged the dangers of this practice as well. In Chapter 6, we referenced a compliance study conducted by the U.S. Securities and Exchange Commission (SEC) in November 2015. One of the best practices noted by the SEC was that the CCO had sufficient authority to influence adherence to compliance policies and procedures. Independent CCO reporting lines are considered critical to this authority. Exhibit 10.1 demonstrates examples of commingled and independent reporting structures.

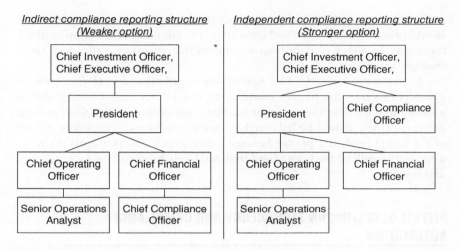

EXHIBIT 10.1 Comparison of Independent and Indirect Compliance Reporting Structures

PITFALL 4: OUTSOURCING ALL COMPLIANCE

Hedge funds have a wide variety of third-party support services available to them to assist in managing their compliance obligations. Many hedge funds, in particular smaller or newly launched funds, run the risk of leaning too heavily on these services providers and relinquish all material ownership of compliance themselves.

As we noted in Chapter 6, one area in which a hedge fund may seek to heavily leverage on a third party to assist with compliance is the naming of an outsourced CCO.

Although there are both pros and cons to this practice, and, indeed, it may be a perfectly acceptable solution for certain hedge funds, one of the major risks is that the hedge fund will simply approach the compliance function as a check-the-box exercise, thinking that the outsourced CCO will be entirely responsible for running the compliance function. Regulators, such as the SEC, have noted that hiring an outsourced CCO does not remove the hedge fund's obligations to be an active participant in working with the outsourced CCO to implement and manage a rigorous compliance program.

When using an outsourced CCO model, if a hedge fund mistakenly feels that it must no longer be involved in compliance then it is not uncommon for key compliance risks to be overlooked. The reasons for this include that third parties may have limited day-to-day oversight of a fund's operations and trading activities, which may affect the required compliance measures. In addition, when a hedge fund outsources the compliance function entirely, there may be a lack of coordination among the compliance efforts of these multiple service providers.

Even if an in-house CCO is named, the use of other compliance services providers such as compliance consultants, third-party legal counsel, and to a more limited extent the compliance-related services of groups such as fund administrators, should be balanced against the in-house compliance efforts of the hedge fund. If a proper balance is not struck and problems do arise, ultimately it will be the hedge fund that will likely be penalized by regulators and investors.

PITFALL 5: RELYING ON TECHNOLOGY AND COMPLIANCE AUTOMATION

Hedge funds increasingly have a wide variety of information technology solutions and software that can assist in automating oversight of the compliance function. Technology can facilitate monitoring the trade execution and allocation, personal account dealing, and electronic communication functions. Technology is also commonly utilized to carry out additional ongoing compliance responsibilities in areas including employee training and in testing the implementation of compliance policies.

While technology can be very useful in managing the compliance function, overuse of these technologies is a common pitfall. When onboarding these technological solutions, hedge funds typically expend a significant amount of time and money vetting and selecting the appropriate system to perform a particular task. Once implemented, there is a risk that hedge funds will become overly vested in their use and forgo extensive human oversight.

For example, in trade execution surveillance, a hedge fund may hard code compliance restrictions into the firm's trade order management systems. These rules may preclude certain types of trades from being conducted. For example, if a hedge fund was exposed to material nonpublic information (MNPI) regarding a specific security, the compliance department may code a temporary restriction on the hedge fund trading in that security until the conflict is resolved. Once this rule is in place, the compliance function may assume that the system will function properly and move on to other areas. Let us assume, however, that a trader was able to use the order management system to execute a trade in the security that should have been restricted. This could happen, for example, if there was a coding error when logging the restriction. In that case, if the compliance function relied solely on the system to report any potential trades in the restricted security and none were reported, it would be a compliance violation. In cases such as these, the manual oversight and testing on the effectiveness of automated systems could have served as a second line of defense. By combining technology with human oversight it would have further reduced the potential for trading in the restricted security.

Although automation may provide compliance functions with the ability to do more with increased efficiency, hedge funds should seek to avoid blindly relying on such technology without allocating the appropriate human resources to compliment the technology and provide manual oversight redundancies.

PITFALL 6: LETTING INVESTOR OPINION DRIVE COMPLIANCE PRIORITIES

Although minimum compliance obligations are traditionally overseen by financial regulators, hedge funds maintain a vested interest in ensuring that their investors are satisfied. As we introduced in Chapter 8, investors have increasingly become more educated about hedge fund compliance risks and have enhanced their due diligence efforts. As a result, investors are increasingly pressuring hedge funds not only to pursue minimum regulatory compliance but also to strive for best practice compliance. While admirable, in certain cases, this pressure can create a disconnect between the areas of compliance a hedge fund should actually focus on based on their knowledge of their day-to-day compliance risks and the perceived areas investors feel they should focus on.

Consider the areas of regulatory reporting and cybersecurity. Assume that we have a hedge fund—we will call it Jason Capital Management—that has completed its most recent filings with the SEC; it was a time-intensive and manual process. The hedge fund has decided that this was not efficient and has discussed internally beginning a search for a software solution to facilitate the data collection and formatting necessary to make the reporting process more efficient in the future.

Let us also assume that, at the same time, a well-publicized cyberattack takes place on a different, well-known hedge fund. As a result of the attacks well-publicized nature, both a large majority of prospective and existing investors in Jason Capital Management heard about the cyberattack. Not surprisingly, the issue of cybersecurity becomes one of prominent discussion during subsequent investor due diligence meetings. In some cases, existing investors have strongly suggested that Jason Capital Management increase its efforts in this area including performing more frequent penetration testing and enhancing its cyber defenses. These same investors, in large part, had not voiced any previous concerns regarding Jason Capital Management's cybersecurity policies and procedures. Furthermore, when the cyberattack occurred at the other hedge fund, Jason Capital Management was not affected and the firm has not experienced any cybersecurity issues since then. Understandably, however, when investors read about problems such as this at one hedge fund they begin to put pressure on the hedge funds they are either invested in, or are considering making an investment in, to make sure nothing similar happens.

Ideally, the hedge fund would be able to perform a search for a regulatory reporting software vendor and address the cybersecurity concerns of its investors at the same time. In many cases, this is not practical. Hedge funds may have limited budgets for such projects and in regard to the compliance budget of the firm, the money would likely be better spent addressing the regulatory reporting issue first. Furthermore, because the hedge fund cybersecurity policies and procedures are not deficient, it may be ill advised for the fund to rush out and conduct hasty upgrades without fully vetting the options available for cybersecurity enhancements.

As this example demonstrates, the disconnect between what compliance priorities may actually be best for the firm and what investors may want can create compliance management challenges for hedge funds. While certainly hedge funds should engage in open dialogues with investors and be responsive to their feedback in the area of compliance, they should also be cautious that they are not led off course from effectively managing compliance priorities in order to minimize the overall compliance risks to the firm.

CHAPTER SUMMARY

This chapter provided an overview of common compliance risk areas facing hedge funds. We began with a discussion of the compliance pitfalls facing many newly launched and smaller hedge funds seeking to build compliance infrastructures that are not appropriately geared for their smaller size. We then addressed an ongoing challenge for both large and small hedge funds: the underspending on compliance in areas that include training and cybersecurity. Next, we outlined the risks facing hedge funds with regard to maintaining independence in compliance reporting structures. Other common compliance pitfalls highlighted in this chapter included the temptation for a hedge fund to entirely outsource compliance and overreliance on compliance technology. Finally, we addressed the challenges hedge funds face in seeking to balance internal compliance priorities alongside increasing investor compliance demands.

Now that we have furthered our understanding of common compliance challenges facing hedge funds, in the next chapter, we will continue to focus on the real-world application of compliance through interviews with hedge fund compliance service providers.

NOTES

1. Amanda Williams, "Hedge Fund Lost £740,000 in an Apparent Friday Afternoon Fraud Where Conmen Trick People Who Have One Eye on the Weekend," *DailyMail.com*, July 8, 2015.
2. Kit Chellel, "A London Hedge Fund Lost $1.2 Million in a Friday Afternoon Phone Scam," *Bloomberg*, July 7, 2015.
3. Jon Shazar, "Ex-Hedge Fund CFO Glad He Didn't Also Help Nigerian Prince Complete His Wire Transfer," *DealBreaker*, July 8, 2015.
4. Fiona Hamilton, "Hedge Fund Loses £740,000 in 'Friday Fraud,'" *The Times*, July 8, 2015.

CHAPTER 11

Interviews with Compliance Service Providers

INTRODUCTION

To gain better perspective of the real-world applications of hedge fund compliance, this chapter features interviews with representatives of two hedge fund compliance service providers. Each interview focuses on different aspects of the compliance process. When reading through these interviews, it is important to remember the increasingly integral part played by service providers in not only supporting the initial creation of a hedge fund's compliance infrastructure, but facilitating its ongoing management as well.

INTERVIEW WITH KENT WEGRZYN (ACA COMPLIANCE GROUP)

The first interview is with Kent Wegrzyn of ACA Compliance Group (ACA). ACA is a leading provider of regulatory compliance products and solutions, cybersecurity, and risk assessments, performance services, and technology solutions to regional, national, and global firms in the financial services industry.

Mr. Wegrzyn joined ACA in 2007. He currently serves as a Managing Director and Hedge Fund Practice Leader in the firm's Chicago office. As Co-Leader of ACA's Hedge Fund Practice, Kent contributes to ACA's hedge fund product development and sales initiative efforts and to building out ACA's hedge fund infrastructure and subject-matter expertise. He also provides regulatory compliance consulting to clients that range from hedge fund start-ups to firms with over $5 billion in assets under management (AUM). Along with these activities, Kent consults with private equity firms and traditional investment managers on compliance with federal securities laws. He prepares investment firms for U.S. Securities and Exchange Commission (SEC) registration and conducts mock SEC inspections to help these firms identify and address their unique compliance and operational risks. In addition, Kent plays an integral role on ACA's business development team and speaks frequently at financial industry events.

Prior to joining ACA, Kent served as a securities compliance examiner at the SEC's Chicago office, where he was hired under the federal government's Outstanding Scholar Program. While at the SEC, he led and/or participated in over 50 examinations of investment advisers, hedge funds, and investment companies. Several of these exams prompted referrals to the SEC's Division of Enforcement, the Internal Revenue Service, and the U.S. Attorney General for further investigation. While at the SEC, Kent also led discussions with other regional offices involving novel hedge fund issues. Kent earned his bachelor's degree in finance from the University of Illinois at Urbana–Champaign. He has also been awarded the Chartered Alternative Investment Analyst designation and is a member of the CAIA Association.

Compliance Consultant Services

Mr. Scharfman: Can you provide an overview of the types of services a hedge fund compliance consultant, such as ACA Compliance Group, performs for a hedge fund as it prepares to launch?

Mr. Wegrzyn: Compliance consultants are very experienced in building out compliance programs for start-up hedge fund managers. A first step is to identify the various rules and regulations the firm will be subject to. The hedge fund manager's location, AUM, marketing activities, and investment strategy will dictate whether the firm will be regulated by one or more of the regulators, including the Securities and Exchange Commission (SEC), the Financial Conduct Authority (FCA), the Financial Industry Regulatory Authority (FINRA), the National Futures Association (NFA), and/or other regulators.

Compliance consultants often assist start-up firms through the relevant registration process. Registering as an investment adviser with the SEC entails drafting application and disclosure documents, such as Form ADV Part 1A, 2A, and 2B. Compliance consultants also assist with the drafting of compliance policies and procedures, which should be customized to address relevant operational, compliance, and business risks. During and after the compliance policies and procedures are drafted, consultants can work with the Chief Compliance Officer (CCO) to train employees on their roles and responsibilities under the compliance program. In addition, it's important for hedge funds to perform a record-keeping gap analysis to ensure that the firm can maintain the relevant books and records required under Rule 204-2 of the Investment Advisers Act of 1940 (Advisers Act). Finally, consultants can assist in the development and implementation of a compliance calendar to ensure the firm stays on top of important compliance and regulatory deadlines.

Mr. Scharfman: What additional services are typically provided after a hedge fund launches?

Mr. Wegrzyn: Compliance consultants are typically engaged to provide consulting on an ongoing basis to answer day-to-day compliance and operational questions. In addition, consultants are engaged to perform annual compliance program reviews, which are required for registered investment advisers under Rule 206(4)-7 of the Advisers Act. Standard engagements for ongoing consulting services also include compliance manual support, reviews of marketing materials and advertisements, regulatory filings support, compliance education and training, electronic correspondence reviews and surveillance, regulatory inspection support, personal account trading compliance assistance, and periodic on-site CCO support.

Mr. Scharfman: Can you provide some perspective on the importance of testing compliance policies and procedures once they are implemented? What services would a compliance consultant offer in this regard?

Mr. Wegrzyn: Adequate testing of compliance policies and procedures is critical to ensure the compliance program is functioning properly. Compliance consultants not only help firms build out comprehensive testing programs they also can be engaged to perform the testing. A typical testing matrix includes a description of each compliance risk, the relevant control policy, the testing procedures, the frequency of the testing, the responsible party, the completion dates, the results, and the action plan. Certain areas of the compliance program need to be tested more frequently than others. For example, personal trading surveillance should be completed at least quarterly.

Mr. Scharfman: What services are typically performed on-site versus ongoing off-site surveillance?

Mr. Wegrzyn: It is important to consider the depth of the testing performed. Hedge fund managers should do more than just "check the box" and should consider updating their testing program on a periodic basis to account for changes in their business activities and new regulations. Testing can be performed on-site or off-site so long as the compliance consultant has access to the appropriate records and personnel.

Mr. Scharfman: Some hedge funds do not utilize compliance consultants. Do you feel that all hedge funds could benefit from using a compliance consultant? If so, why?

Mr. Wegrzyn: Yes, we believe that all hedge fund advisers can benefit from engaging an independent third party to conduct ongoing work and/or one-off projects. Compliance consulting firms have services designed to add value for hedge fund advisers, ranging from start-ups to mid-size to firms managing over $100 billion. For example, small to mid-size hedge fund advisers often rely on the expertise of compliance consulting firms to conduct much of the "heavy lifting" of a compliance program, while very large hedge fund advisers often utilize compliance consultants for project work such as focused mock audits.

Certainly, firms that have a dedicated internal audit or in-house compliance testing function would require the services of a compliance consultant less often. However, we find that internal compliance personnel at hedge fund firms often do not have the resources or expertise to perform comprehensive compliance reviews. Since one of the main responsibilities of compliance consultants is to stay up-to-date on regulatory developments, industry best practices, and regulatory expectations, they can bring a unique perspective that leads them to identify undetected compliance issues and enhancement opportunities. A good compliance consultant has his "finger on the pulse" with respect to current regulatory and industry practices.

Mr. Scharfman: How has the role of compliance consultants to hedge funds evolved over the last five years?

Mr. Wegrzyn: The use of compliance consultants is now mainstream, especially since many hedge fund managers continue to maintain lean operational frameworks. CCOs within smaller hedge fund organizations typically wear multiple hats (e.g., CFO, COO), which makes it difficult from a resource standpoint to test and implement the compliance program internally. In addition, regulators are getting more aggressive, which is contributing to the increased use of compliance consultants.

Interaction with Other Hedge Fund Service Providers and Compliance Consultants

Mr. Scharfman: How do compliance consultants typically interact with other hedge fund service providers, such as law firms, fund administrators, prime brokers, and auditors?

Mr. Wegrzyn: A good compliance consultancy should be able to address relevant regulatory and operational issues taking place at their hedge fund clients but will refer legal concerns to counsel. In certain situations, such as when a hedge fund manager is preparing new policies and procedures, firms may wish to have their compliance consultants draft the documents and ask their attorneys to review them as an additional control or vice versa. Compliance consultants don't often work closely with administrators, prime brokers, or auditors, but in the course of carrying out compliance testing, conducting annual reviews, or providing regulatory advice, may occasionally interview these parties or review their work product.

Mr. Scharfman: Some hedge funds invest and raise capital in multiple countries. If a hedge fund does business in multiple countries, such as the United States and U.K., how does that change the way it works with a compliance consultant?

Mr. Wegrzyn: Developments in financial regulation and the extraterritorial nature of recent legislation have resulted in managers who conduct business internationally having to register their funds and/or the management entity with regulatory bodies outside of the jurisdiction in which they are based.

Previously, managers had been comfortable in utilizing the regulatory consulting services of a boutique provider for local matters, but as a result of the above, we have seen a material shift in the market's approach to compliance and regulation. With professional and corporate reputation at risk and personal liability at stake, the market now demands a provider that has the knowledge, experience, and stability to service clients with international or global requirements.

Mr. Scharfman: If different compliance consultants are utilized for each country or region, what advice would you give a hedge fund seeking to coordinate the efforts of two different consultants?

Mr. Wegrzyn: As discussed above, it is now a relatively rare occurrence that a manager will engage with a compliance consultancy that cannot service all or at least the majority of the markets in which it has regulatory obligations, hence the growth of ACA internationally. However, where a manager is, either by legacy or choice, engaged with multiple providers, we would recommend relationships that have a clearly defined scope and are transparent from a communications perspective. All of the providers in the structure should possess a clear understanding of their respective roles, responsibilities, timings, and limitations.

Where possible, it would also help to engage firms that do not have competing services since this can make a significant difference in relationship management and the prevention of conflicts of interest. Finally, from the outset, a decision should be made on how global compliance policies, procedures, and accompanying documentation will take account of and address a variety of regulatory obligations in different jurisdictions and which consultant will take the lead in this effort. To conclude, a multiple provider structure would require careful planning, conflict management, and the allocation of an internal relationship manager to ensure all parties are working cohesively toward mutually agreed upon objectives.

Mr. Scharfman: What is your perspective relating to the practice of certain hedge funds that use other service providers, such as law firms, as opposed to traditional compliance consultants, for compliance-related work in areas such as compliance training?

Mr. Wegrzyn: It is quite common for hedge funds to engage both outside legal counsel and compliance consultants for compliance-related work, including training sessions. Law firms may be engaged to provide specific training sessions to employees regarding insider trading and the legal intricacies involved with determining whether information is considered material and nonpublic.

A good compliance consultant will focus not only on the letter of the law and federal regulations but also on how regulators may interpret certain issues, what other managers are doing to address those issues, and how the firm may run its business from an operations perspective in order to meet regulatory expectations. Hedge fund managers should decide whether to use a law firm or a consultancy (or both) based on their own businesses and priorities.

Mr. Scharfman: There has been a growing trend in recent years of non-compliance-focused service providers, such as fund administrators, offering hedge funds compliance-related services, such as assistance with regulatory reporting for Form PF in the United States. In your opinion, how should hedge funds evaluate these offerings for compliance-related services from non-compliance-focused firms?

Mr. Wegrzyn: Certain service providers, including fund administrators, may have easy access to very detailed information necessary to complete certain filings. As you noted, Form PF is the most obvious of these. There may be value in utilizing non-compliance firms for such purposes, but they may not approach the engagement with a focus on regulatory considerations. For this reason, hedge fund managers should consider asking their compliance consultants to perform a reasonableness review of these deliverables.

Mr. Scharfman: Do you feel there is a benefit to consolidating these types of services at a compliance consultant?

Mr. Wegrzyn: Yes, there is certainly a benefit to consolidation. For example, if a manager can have one firm produce a draft of its Form PF filing and simultaneously address associated regulatory considerations, a timely filing can be made with fewer administrative steps and fewer parties involved. ACA's Technology Division has created software that is capable of automatically generating responses to the questions on Form PF, and our consulting staff, the members of which are generally familiar with this system, can then review the output for regulatory concerns. Consolidation may also help advisers save on related fees.

Mr. Scharfman: An area of increasing importance for hedge funds from a compliance perspective is vendor due diligence. What are some best practices in this area and how can a compliance consultant assist in this process?

Mr. Wegrzyn: Hedge fund managers should first identify the vendors that pose the biggest risk, such as those that have access to sensitive investor or proprietary information and those that are involved in critical business operations. Next, firms should implement procedures for conducting initial and ongoing due diligence of their vendors and should start with the high-risk vendors and work their way down.

Consultants can assist with the development of a vendor due diligence review process, test that firms are executing due diligence review processes, point out compliance gaps in the diligence processes, and provide suggested enhancements. It is also very important that firms review vendors from a cybersecurity perspective. Cybersecurity consultants can perform the actual due diligence of vendors on a firm's behalf. Such diligence is tremendously important to ensure that a firm does not compromise its proprietary or investor information.

Governance

Mr. Scharfman: What role do you feel a hedge fund's in-house compliance department and its compliance consultants may play in relation to governance?

Mr. Wegrzyn: Internal compliance personnel and external consultants often play a limited role, if any, in the governance of the actual funds. This is in contrast to mutual funds and other registered investment companies that have various compliance-reporting obligations to the fund's board of directors. With regard to the governance of fund managers, this will vary from firm to firm. In smaller firms, the CCO may often be an owner or member of senior management, in which case they will participate in the governance of the firm through that position if not their compliance role. In larger firms, it is rare for the CCO to participate in the overall governance of the firm. However, they will often report directly to senior management or a member thereof, and they may be able to influence governance indirectly, depending on the amount of autonomy they have over the firm's compliance program.

At minimum, the SEC expects a hedge fund adviser's CCO to be empowered with full responsibility and authority to develop and enforce appropriate policies and procedures for the adviser. To our knowledge, compliance consultants play no role in the governance of fund advisers, except to the extent the adviser acts upon the consultant's recommendations.

Mr. Scharfman: What interaction, if any, does a compliance consultant typically have with a hedge fund's board of directors?

Mr. Wegrzyn: From time to time, SEC examiners will ask to interview the independent directors of offshore hedge funds. Compliance consultants may therefore ask to do the same when conducting mock examinations and compliance program reviews.

Mr. Scharfman: Similarly, what interaction with boards may be in place at a hedge fund, not at the individual fund level, but as governance advisory boards at the management company?

Mr. Wegrzyn: Compliance consultants will frequently interview members of senior management when conducting mock exams and compliance program reviews. These interviews may be conducted to obtain a feel for "tone at the top" and/or to obtain information about certain aspects of the firm's business practices and compliance program, to the extent such person plays a role in those activities—members of senior management may have day-to-day responsibilities and/or sit on committees, such as investment, best execution, or valuation committees. Further, consultants may be asked to present their findings directly to senior management rather than or in addition to a firm's compliance personnel.

Mr. Scharfman: What trends are you seeing in regard to the relationship between hedge fund governance and compliance?

Mr. Wegrzyn: Offshore fund directors are asking more questions about compliance programs, resources, and deficiencies. We are also noticing a trend of fund adviser senior management taking compliance more seriously.

Regulatory Reporting

Mr. Scharfman: What are the key items hedge funds should be conscious of when approaching regulatory reporting?

Mr. Wegrzyn: Hedge funds should be conscious of the following: (1) knowing those regulatory reports that they are or may be required to make, (2) monitoring their calendar and activities to ensure that such reports are made on a timely basis, and (3) ensuring that such reports are accurately compiled.

Regarding item 1, there are multiple regulatory reports about which hedge fund advisers should be cognizant. Some reports will apply to most if not all advisers, whereas others will only be relevant if a fund has certain characteristics or engages in certain activities. For example, any U.S. fund adviser with regulatory assets of more than $150 million will ultimately need to file Forms ADV and PF, but only funds that short sell EU securities need to worry about filing reports under European Short Selling Regulation (EU) No. 236/2012.

With regard to timing, some "routine" regulatory reports are subject to set deadlines that rarely change, but deadlines for other reports will be determined by the event that necessitates the filing. For example, Form ADV must always be filed within 90 days of an adviser's fiscal year end, whereas a deadline under the European Short Selling Regulation is determined by the date on which the adviser came to hold a triggering short position in a relevant EU security. It is therefore vitally important that funds not only know what event necessitates a reporting obligation, but when such an event has occurred.

Regulatory reports vary in complexity. Form 13F is often relatively straightforward to file but something like Form PF—especially for advisers to hedge funds with net assets of $500 million or more—can be difficult and time consuming to complete. In order to accurately file the more complicated regulatory reports, fund managers should ensure that they both: (1) understand the questions being asked of them and (2) have the necessary data and expertise to answer such questions.

Mr. Scharfman: What are some of the common mistakes you see managers make in this area?

Mr. Wegrzyn: We rarely see managers fail to make "routine" filings on a timely basis, although this happens occasionally. One of the greatest risks is when circumstances change or a manager does something for the first time, and the manager is not aware that the change or their actions have triggered a reporting obligation. Even in the case of "routine" filings, there are some questions that certain advisers answer incorrectly. For example, certain advisers do not follow the SEC's instructions for calculating regulatory AUM when completing Form ADV and instead use their own methodology for this purpose.

Mr. Scharfman: How do you feel hedge funds have addressed the AIFMD Annex IV reporting? How do you feel this compares to the response for Form PF filing in the United States?

Mr. Wegrzyn: From an operational standpoint, in our view, firms have approached Annex IV in much the same way as other systemic risk reports, such as Form PF. This type of reporting typically requires input across multiple business units and also third-party service providers (in some cases, the latter, assuming day-to-day responsibility for the initial preparation of the filings and following internal review and sign off of their submission).

Form PF reporting is, at this stage, far more established, as it has been in place since 2012, and so far, fewer ambiguities remain surrounding definitions and presentation of data than compared with the newer AIFMD Annex IV. However, these interpretative issues have largely bedded down for firms that have undertaken multiple cycles of these submissions, and ordinarily, such firms will have sought transparency, volunteering assumptions (through the inclusion of explanatory narrative) that clarify their approach when applying the available guidance to their AIF structure. In relation to both types of reporting, the onus is on firms to maintain their awareness of subsequent guidance issued by the relevant regulators that may affect their reporting obligations.

For Annex IV reporting, in which a non-EU Manager has filed to market in multiple European Economic Area (EEA) member states, the principal difference in comparison to Form PF is having to grapple with different juris-dictional interpretations that may impact the volume of data required (with some EEA regulators requiring Master Fund data for any feeder funds mar-keted in their territory but most not) as well as navigating various submission mechanisms, ranging from online portals to secure file transfer.

Mr. Scharfman: What trends do you expect to see in the future with regard to regulatory reporting?

Mr. Wegrzyn: While we cannot predict the future, it is possible that various regulators will increase hedge fund reporting requirements to some extent or another. By way of illustration, on March 25, 2016, FINRA announced changes to Form PF that significantly increased the reporting obligations of liquidity fund advisers. These changes will apply to all filings made following the second quarter of 2016. While these changes will not affect hedge fund advisers, it is possible that comparable changes could be made to the hedge fund sections of Form PF upon similar notice.

Regulatory Audits

Mr. Scharfman: What trends are you seeing with regard to regulatory exam-inations of hedge funds?

Mr. Wegrzyn: During the last two years of the SEC's look into the private fund industry (the "Presence Exam initiative"), the SEC's Office of Compli-ance Inspections and Examinations (OCIE) made various strategic hires in the creation of the Private Funds Unit (PFU). As a result, we've seen OCIE become more efficient in scoping examination candidates, enhancing exami-nation plans, and staffing examinations. A direct result of the Presence Exam initiative is the use of shorter initial document request lists with OCIE exam-iners taking a deep-dive look into one to three areas that may create the biggest risk at a hedge fund firm.

The SEC has developed certain efficiencies/economies of scale to address the mountains of new data coming in from hedge fund advisers. With changes to Form ADV and the implementation of Form PF, the industry is witnessing three divisions in the SEC—the Division of Economic and Risk Analysis (DERA), the Division of Investment Management (IM), and OCIE—work together like never before to use data to target specific market conduct or other thematic ideas.

Over the past several years, the SEC has started to publicize current focus areas with the release of OCIE's annual examination priorities. We've seen OCIE executives give speeches on certain trends or themes arising out of recently concluded examinations as well as announcements that examiners will focus on certain new types of deficient conduct going forward.

Mr. Scharfman: What are the primary benefits of having a mock audit performed by a third party?

Mr. Wegrzyn: We believe there are many benefits to a mock examination. Chief among them is that the firm can make a reasonable judgment about its state of preparedness for the eventuality that is an SEC examination. Specifically, an appropriately tailored and staffed mock examination can provide the firm with an independent view of:

- How the hedge fund manager handled the production of documents from the initial request through the final supplemental request for information
- How the hedge fund manager's staff—from the CEO of the firm to the most recently hired analyst—handled questions about roles, responsibilities, documents specific to the interviewee's role, and understanding of the firm's compliance obligations
- How the hedge fund manager addresses the current regulatory environment, including industry norms or best practices
- How the hedge fund manager defines, detects, and mitigates conflicts of interest
- Gaps in the hedge fund manager's level of compliance with SEC rules, no-action guidance, and/or any investor mandated reporting obligations
- Ideas, solutions, or other recommendations for rectifying any weaknesses noted during the mock examination

Mr. Scharfman: With what frequency do you recommend a hedge fund undergo such a review?

Mr. Wegrzyn: Many small and midsize advisers outsource the annual compliance program review to third parties. With the SEC analyzing data gleaned from certain regulatory filings to aid its deployment of a risk-based approach to determining examination candidates, we would generally recommend that an adviser consider a mock examination or third-party compliance review every one to three years. There are a few reasons for this:

1. Regulatory oversight changes. With Dodd-Frank causing much of the private fund industry to register with a regulatory body for the first time, we saw the SEC take issue with what were previously thought to be standard industry practices (for example, how private equity firms have been challenged with expense allocations, advisory fee issues, and other disclosure-related items). Even if the SEC does not undertake additional rule makings or issues other guidance, industry best practice is ever evolving and consistently being probed by the SEC.
2. Examination cycles change. The SEC exam program is continually evolving. Specifically, the SEC is developing additional tools, methodologies, and tactics to speed up the manner in which it conducts

examinations. One could reasonably assume that risk-based testing combined with new tools and additional hires would allow the SEC to conduct a greater amount of examinations every year.
3. Investor demand. While certain large institutional investors may have staff capable of taking on the diligence necessary to vet a hedge fund manager, many investors have started to request that hedge fund managers undertake regular mock examinations to provide some assurance that the firm they're investing with maintains a culture of compliance and does not have items of concern that could create regulatory headaches.

Mr. Scharfman: Some investors may encounter hedge funds that have never undergone a third-party mock audit. Common reasons funds provide for this is that it is not cost effective, it is too much a burden on internal resources to perform such a review, and that funds may perform their own internal compliance testing, which obviates the need to engage a third party to perform a mock audit. How would you respond to these common objections to third-party mock audits?

Mr. Wegrzyn: While we acknowledge that a mock examination can place some stress on a manager and its staff, including the stresses of dealing with competing organizational priorities, document production, and interviews, we believe firms get significant value from a well-scoped and staffed mock examination. With a mock examination, the compliance department gets the opportunity to preview how the rest of a firm would conduct itself during the course of an SEC examination, including the performance of its personnel in gathering documents and undergoing interviews with SEC examiners. How a hedge fund manager handles the examination process can affect the SEC's findings and the length of the examination.

Mr. Scharfman: What perspective would you give to investors in evaluating the regulatory audit risks associated with these funds?

Mr. Wegrzyn: Our hedge fund clients that have gone through an ACA mock audit tend to perform much better during actual regulatory examinations. Not only was ACA the brainchild of four former SEC examiners and one state examiner, ACA's continued focus is the recruitment/hiring of SEC examiners as well as professionals who have served in compliance roles at a range of firms and asset classes. These professionals, who have sat on both sides of the regulatory examination table, give ACA a unique insight and perspective on regulatory issues and trends that few firms have.

Chief Compliance Officer

Mr. Scharfman: What is your perspective on hedge funds that may utilize an outsourced Chief Compliance Officer?

Mr. Wegrzyn: For a small firm with a relatively simple business model that does not have the resources to be able to hire an effective/adequate/experienced CCO, the outsourced CCO model may be useful. However, we believe there is no substitute for having a competent and empowered employee with appropriate seniority to serve as a firm's CCO. Even if this person is multi-hatted, they will be intimately aware of the firm's operations and can help ensure there is an ethical environment as well as a culture of compliance.

Based on the recent proposal to amend Form ADV (Release No. IA-4091) and OCIE's release of a risk alert (Vol. 5, No. 1) highlighting the examination staff's observations of firms that use an outsourced CCO, the SEC seems to believe the practice is worth monitoring on an ongoing basis. If the proposed amendments are adopted, the SEC will capture information regarding whether a CCO is compensated or employed by another firm, among other things. The release also indicates that the proposed amendments would allow the SEC to further assess potential risks, which could mean hedge fund advisers using an outsourced CCO will fall higher on the SEC's internal risk ranking tool used to determine examination candidates.

With regard to the SEC's sweep examination that culminated in the release of the aforementioned risk alert, the SEC highlighted certain issues resulting directly from the use of an outsourced CCO as well as some cautionary language to firms that currently use or are considering such an arrangement.

Mr. Scharfman: In general, at what level of AUM threshold do you feel it is appropriate for a hedge fund to begin maintaining dedicated in-house compliance staff to complement the work of any third-party compliance consultants?

Mr. Wegrzyn: AUM is just one of the factors that should be evaluated when determining whether a firm should have in-house compliance staff. The complexity of the firm as a whole needs to be evaluated, including the types and number of investment strategies, the number of clients/funds, the financial affiliations of the hedge fund manager, the number of employees and office locations, and whether the firm has been involved in previous regulatory issues.

At a minimum, a hedge fund manager should have a named internal CCO. Many firms earmark resources to engage outside consultants and/or outside counsel to supplement the CCO's need for additional expertise in running an effective compliance program. Engaging a third party to conduct periodic mock examinations or to provide ongoing consulting is an effective way for a CCO to determine whether the firm can mitigate any foot faults or larger issues before the SEC announces an examination.

Mr. Scharfman: An issue that has recently been increasingly debated relates to the liability of a hedge fund's CCO for compliance violations. What is your perspective on CCO liability?

Mr. Wegrzyn: The SEC has come out publicly to state that it is not targeting CCOs. However, these comments came on the heels of the SEC's announcement of two settled cases whereby the CCO was specifically named in the enforcement actions. We believe the SEC will continue to pursue CCOs who are directly involved in misconduct, who attempted to mislead the SEC staff, or who completely failed to carry out their responsibilities as CCOs. Further, CCO cases could have a chilling effect on how a CCO drafts policies and procedures or how a firm's CCO carries out oversight of the firm's activities.

Mr. Scharfman: What role do you feel compliance consultants can play in this regard?

Mr. Wegrzyn: In this era where both OCIE and the SEC's Division of Enforcement have specialized in evaluating certain types of firms, hedge fund advisers included, compliance consulting firms can be extremely useful to a hedge fund adviser's compliance program. During the course of a relationship with a compliance consultant such as ACA, a hedge fund adviser can reap the benefits of a business partner that is proactive in staying on top of SEC guidance, proposed/finalized rule makings, as well as changes, both announced and subtle, to the way the SEC conducts its examinations.

Through a relationship that entails both ongoing consulting as well as an annual mock examination, CCOs will benefit immensely by learning more about the firm's operations through the mock examination interviews with senior/junior employees; reviews and testing of policies and procedures; ongoing guidance and advisement toward best practices resulting from the consulting firm's work with peer firms; and the ability to identify and mitigate the issues typically cited by SEC examiners before a formal examination takes place.

Use of Technology in Compliance

Mr. Scharfman: In regard to the compliance function, what trends are you seeing with the use of technology by hedge funds and their compliance consultants?

Mr. Wegrzyn: The use of technology across the board has continued to increase. Hedge funds and compliance consultants are constantly looking at technology solutions to assist with various compliance and operational tasks, especially for firms that engage in active trading.

For example, hedge funds are utilizing technology for, among other things, personal trading reporting and monitoring, preclearance requests, restricted list testing, investment guidelines and restrictions, e-mail reviews, regulatory filing obligations, and trade surveillance.

Mr. Scharfman: Can you comment on how you feel hedge fund CCOs who may not have extensive backgrounds in information technology (IT) should approach the increasing role of the compliance department in technology-focused areas, such as cybersecurity? How can compliance consultants assist?

Mr. Wegrzyn: Technology has become an area that CCOs must embrace. While CCOs are not expected to be experts in technology, they should have enough technological knowledge to determine whether their firm should bring on expertise in particular areas, such as cybersecurity. In addition, it is essential that CCOs maintain an open line of communication with IT and hold periodic meetings to go over firm initiatives and relevant regulatory guidance and industry best practices related to IT.

Compliance consultants can provide another layer of assistance to CCOs with regard to technology and specifically cybersecurity. For example, certain compliance consultants, ACA included, have expanded their reach by adding experts that focus exclusively on hedge fund–related technology and cybersecurity issues. These technology experts evaluate various IT controls and practices as well as conduct tests on technological systems to ensure sufficient controls are in place. For example, these experts are able to, among other things, run penetration and phishing tests, holistic risk assessments, and internal and external network testing. By teaming up with technology experts, compliance consultants are able to ease the concerns of CCOs that lack IT backgrounds.

Mr. Scharfman: What compliance challenges and trends are you seeing with hedge funds' increasing use of social media?

Mr. Wegrzyn: The world is becoming more and more technical in nature and the way people communicate in everyday life is changing from telephonic and in-person meetings to social networking, texting, messaging, and the like. With that come challenges not only from a record-keeping perspective but also from a monitoring perspective as well.

Although many firms prohibit their employees from using social media for the purpose of fund-raising or marketing, just communicating informally through these means with business contacts may require the firm to maintain and monitor the correspondence. Because of this, firms are identifying the use of social media as a higher-risk area and periodically testing employees' compliance with the firm's policies in this area. Due to the time-intensive nature of this monitoring, we are seeing hedge fund managers rely on third-party consultants to test compliance with social media policies.

Mr. Scharfman: For legacy or cost reasons, not every hedge fund embraces the extensive use of technology in compliance. For example, some hedge funds may collect paper copies of brokerage statements to oversee employee personal account trading. What advice would you offer to hedge funds still utilizing these types of paper-based approaches?

Mr. Wegrzyn: These firms should consider embracing technology to streamline processes and to make their operations more efficient. Personal trading policies and procedures should be designed to eliminate concerns of front running, insider trading, and trading opposite of clients, among other things. Testing these risk areas is substantially more difficult when receiving paper copies of employee brokerage statements. If the paper-based approach is used for personal trading reviews, it is important to consider the following items:

- All statements must be dated upon receipt to ensure they are received within the time frames established by Rule 204A-1.
- Compliance should perform thorough reviews of all personal trading statements to ensure compliance with the Code of Ethics, especially pre-clearance requirements.
- Compliance should sign or provide some other documentation to evidence their review of all employees' brokerage statements.
- All statements should be stored in a locked filing cabinet.
- Watch lists and/or restricted lists must be periodically provided to employees to avoid any personal trading in the names on either list.

Mr. Scharfman: What perspective would you offer to investors seeking to evaluate the compliance risks associated with hedge funds that underutilize technology in this area?

Mr. Wegrzyn: In these cases, investors should thoroughly review the hedge fund manager's code of ethics and personal trading guidelines. If employees are permitted to trade in the same or similar names or even the same industry as the hedge fund, then investors should be wary of additional compliance risks. For example, front running and trading opposite of client accounts could occur throughout the quarter, and without a technological system in place, such trades would not be flagged until the end of the quarter.

Furthermore, with regard to the hedge fund manager's code of ethics, investors should evaluate whether a restricted list and/or watch list is utilized as well as if any holding or blackout periods are warranted on personal trading. Investors should evaluate how these practices are implemented on a manual basis as they are commonly found in technology systems that other hedge fund managers use to monitor personal trading.

Compliance Expense Management

Mr. Scharfman: With increasing compliance demands in areas such as regulatory reporting, the cost of compliance for hedge funds globally has increased in recent years. Are there any general guidelines to how much (i.e., a percentage of AUM) is the average or appropriate for a hedge fund to spend on compliance annually?

Mr. Wegrzyn: The amount of compliance spending really depends on the size and complexity of the hedge fund manager. Specific factors that play into the decision include the amount of AUM, the types and number of investment strategies, the number of clients/funds, the financial affiliations of the hedge fund manager, the number of employees and office locations, and whether the firm has been involved in previous regulatory issues.

Mr. Scharfman: In what areas of compliance are you seeing hedge funds increase their compliance budgets?

Mr. Wegrzyn: We are seeing an increase in spending on technology services such as trade surveillance software, regulatory reporting systems, and cybersecurity improvements. The SEC maintains a Quantitative Analytics Unit that has developed an instrument called NEAT, which stands for National Exam Analytics Tool. NEAT allows SEC examiners to access and systematically analyze massive amounts of trading data and searches for evidence of insider trading, market manipulation, front running, improper allocations, and other kinds of misconduct. The hedge fund industry has taken notice and is in the early stages of evaluating trade surveillance vendors that provide services similar to NEAT.

Mr. Scharfman: How can compliance consultants assist in better managing compliance overall expenses?

Mr. Wegrzyn: Compliance consultants can help hedge fund managers perform comprehensive risk assessments. The idea is to identify high-risk items and conflicts of interest that are most pressing within the organization. Each risk can be ranked as high, moderate, or low. CCOs should prioritize their resources on addressing the higher-risk items while working with their compliance consultants to identify the most-efficient and cost-effective manner of addressing the issues.

Hedge Fund Marketing and Compliance

Mr. Scharfman: In recent years, hedge funds have broadened the ways they market themselves to the public, in part due to the loosening of regulatory rules through the passage of legislation, such as the JOBS Act in the United States. What compliance challenges has this posed?

Mr. Wegrzyn: Firms that intend to solicit the general public for investment in their private funds should keep in mind that, pursuant to Rule 506 of Regulation D, they are responsible for taking reasonable steps to verify that all investors in those funds are accredited. Because of this verification obligation, very few hedge fund managers have actually taken advantage of the loosened general solicitation rules. Additionally, the SEC has taken an interest in firms that engage in general solicitation for private offerings under this exemption. We have recently observed certain fund managers who were audited shortly after submitting filings that indicated they planned to engage in general solicitation, so hedge fund managers should be prepared for increased regulatory scrutiny if they opt to go this route.

Mr. Scharfman: In particular, many hedge funds now maintain public websites with more information than they previously had. What is compliance's role in overseeing these types of marketing efforts?

Mr. Wegrzyn: Hedge fund managers that have not explicitly opted to rely on Rule 506(c) and comply with the relevant accreditation requirements should still ensure that their marketing materials, including their websites, do not give the appearance that they are soliciting the public for investments. Compliance should generally be involved in the monitoring of all marketing materials to ensure that applicable advertising restrictions are observed, and firms should consider applying this oversight to website updates as well.

Mr. Scharfman: Countries such as Switzerland have recently revised the rules with the ways non-Swiss hedge funds may be marketed in Switzerland. What role can compliance consultants play in ensuring hedge funds follow international marketing guidelines?

Mr. Wegrzyn: Compliance consultants typically provide a high-level overview of the marketing guidelines (including any restrictions) of international jurisdictions, including those across the EEA and Switzerland (which lies outside the EEA). For a more detailed summary in each jurisdiction, we would advise hedge fund managers to get in touch with local legal counsel. Specifically, with respect to the requirement for a Swiss representative, compliance consultants may also assist by making introductions to such providers.

Additional Questions

Mr. Scharfman: What are some best practices in the ways hedge fund compliance functions should approach the management of insider trading risk?

Mr. Wegrzyn: To manage insider trading risk, it is important to first identify the various sources and avenues from which a firm may receive or come in contact with material, nonpublic information. Examples include meetings with management, consultations with industry consultants, meetings with politicians, idea dinners, sitting on an issuer's creditors committee, and relationships with other hedge fund managers. After this information has been identified, compliance should establish, maintain, and enforce written policies, procedures, and controls reasonably designed to mitigate insider trading risks.

Compliance should also consider conducting periodic education and training sessions for all employees as well as certification of compliance with all insider trading policies and procedures. Additional controls include establishing watch and/or restricted lists, information barriers (if applicable), preclearance requirements, and holding periods as warranted. Last, compliance should perform e-mail reviews and periodic trading surveillance, including testing of both firm and employee trading accounts.

Mr. Scharfman: What about the protection of client data?

Mr. Wegrzyn: To ensure sufficient protection of client data, compliance should work with the IT group to establish written policies and procedures addressing the receipt, delivery, and archival of all client data. Compliance and IT should ensure that only employees that need access to client data for their job responsibilities are granted access. Firms may also consider enhancing their security controls by encrypting client data and adding password requirements to access client data. Hard-copy files of client data should be limited, but in the event hard-copy files are maintained, compliance should ensure such files are kept in locked filing cabinets. Last, compliance in conjunction with IT should provide periodic training to all employees on privacy controls and safeguarding of client data.

Mr. Scharfman: What are best practices in conflict of interest management of employees among a hedge fund's different investment vehicles?

Mr. Wegrzyn: The allocation of investment opportunities can present (material) conflicts of interest when hedge fund managers advise multiple clients/funds. This is particularly relevant if one investment vehicle has a higher incentive allocation than the other vehicle, and/or if the hedge fund manager is running a proprietary account. Compliance should establish formal trade allocation policies and procedures that are designed to treat all clients fairly. Allocations that fall outside the standard policy should be documented with a reason code and should be reviewed and approved by compliance personnel. Compliance personnel and their consultants should also periodically test trade allocations to ensure compliance with the policies and procedures.

Mr. Scharfman: What about in the area of employee political contributions?

Mr. Wegrzyn: Political contributions during an election year give rise to elevated risk. Violating the Pay-to-Play Rule brings serious consequences, including the prohibition of receiving compensation from a government entity for two years following a contribution to an official of that government entity. The most critical part of managing this risk is implementing sound policies and procedures, which should include preclearance requirements. However, like all other areas of the compliance program, hedge fund managers should trust but verify. Compliance personnel and/or their consultants should review preclearance logs and requests and verify such information against publicly available databases of political contributions. Slip-ups may happen intentionally or unintentionally, but catching them before the regulators do is critical and shows a working compliance program.

Mr. Scharfman: What areas of compliance do you feel should be the highest priority for hedge funds in the coming year?

Mr. Wegrzyn: *Fund Expenses*: Hedge fund managers should implement formal policies and procedures to ensure the proper allocation of fund expenses. Compliance and legal personnel should ensure that only those expenses that are explicitly disclosed to investors in the Form ADV and fund governing documents are charged to the funds. We also recommend that hedge fund managers conduct regular testing of their fund expense allocation processes, especially since this has become a focus area of the SEC and investors. Conflicts of interest should be identified and mitigated (e.g., disclosure, change in business practice) to ensure the adviser upholds its fiduciary duty to act in the best interests of clients.

Trade Surveillance: As mentioned above, the SEC has implemented the NEAT tool that allows examiners to access and systematically analyze massive amounts of trading data and search for evidence of insider trading, market manipulation, front running, improper allocations, and other kinds of misconduct. Since these types of misconduct can devastate the reputation of a firm, hedge fund managers should be taking steps to improve their trade surveillance techniques.

Valuation: There have been some recent SEC enforcement cases relating to valuation. Hedge fund managers should ensure they have implemented policies and procedures designed to price investments in a manner that is fair, accurate, and consistent with any disclosures. Compliance personnel should consider paying extra attention to the pricing processes for illiquid securities and should implement a testing program designed to identify potential valuation deficiencies.

Cybersecurity: The SEC and FCA have consistently stressed that firms need to establish and implement effective IT and operational resilience in light of the rising threat of cyber-crime.

Conduct Issues (European/U.K. Issues): Firms must work to implement the new requirements of the EU Market Abuse Regulation (in force since July 3, 2016), especially the specific requirements to prevent, monitor, and report suspicious transactions and orders in relation to market abuse. Firms will also be working to implement the much broader Markets in Financial Instruments Directive and Regulation (together known as MiFID II), which are now due to come into force on January 3, 2018. Of particular relevance to hedge fund managers are specific requirements for best execution and new rules restricting the use of dealing commissions to pay for research.

Mr. Scharfman: Going forward, how do you think the role of compliance consultants will evolve?

Mr. Wegrzyn: With the increasing number of new rules and regulations in the United States and globally, we believe compliance consultants will continue to be relied on to assist hedge fund managers with their compliance obligations and challenges. Compliance consulting expertise can be invaluable when consultants are able to identify compliance issues and recommend practical solutions that meet regulators' expectations.

INTERVIEW WITH VINOD PAUL (EZE CASTLE INTEGRATION)

The second interview is with Vinod Paul of Eze Castle Integration, a leading technology services provider for investment firms worldwide with more than 650 clients spread across three continents.

Mr. Paul is the Managing Director of Service and Business Development. Leading a talented team of customer service and engineering professionals, Mr. Paul oversees all customer-facing engagements for Eze. He joined the company in 2002, and his responsibilities include service delivery and business development for the firm. Previously, he was the director of technical services for Martin Progressive, supervising a staff that supported 6,000 customers. Prior to that, he provided project management and engineering consulting services to IBM Global Services, Lucent Technologies, Tyco Submarine Systems, and Penguin Putnam Publishing. Mr. Paul serves on the board of directors for Hedge Funds Care, a global nonprofit dedicated to supporting efforts to prevent and treat child abuse. He is a graduate of Rutgers University with a bachelor of science degree in biological sciences and holds numerous advanced certifications with Microsoft.

Compliance-Related Information Technology Consultant Services

Mr. Scharfman: For a hedge fund in the process of preparing to launch, what types of compliance-related services would an information technology consultant such as Eze Castle Integration typically perform?

Mr. Paul: An information technology consultant such as Eze Castle Integration plays a key role in assisting a hedge fund during the launch process. One component is providing the underlying technology necessary to meet compliance requirements. We typically assist clients with implementing record retention, message archiving, and disaster recovery solutions as well as helping ensure they have the necessary security safeguards in place.

Cybersecurity is in the spotlight with regulators and the expectations are high. Therefore, we provide clients with IT solutions that include layers of security. These layers include, but are not limited to, antivirus software, host-based and network intrusion detection systems, hardware and software firewalls, encryption, and application filters.

Beyond technical safeguards, we work with launches to create written information security programs that detail the policies and procedures for ensuring confidential data are protected, how it's being protected, and who is ensuring it's protected. This also includes creating an incident response plan, which outlines procedures in the event an incident occurs.

The written policies of a given fund will depend on the size, scale, and nature of a particular fund. At minimum, a set of policies should be able to demonstrate a fund manager has taken reasonable efforts to protect its fund from cybersecurity risks. These policies, if appropriate, can be combined as a collection or incorporated into a compliance manual or employee handbook.

Mr. Scharfman: After a hedge fund has launched, how do information technology consultants typically work with a hedge fund's compliance department?

Mr. Paul: Information technology consultants may work with a hedge fund's compliance department postlaunch on activities that include third-party risk assessments and employee cybersecurity training.

Our firm, for example, helps create employee security awareness curriculum that is tailored to a client's unique business needs, preferences, and policies. The training sessions are often administered as face-to-face, instructor-led, hands-on training. Rather than focusing on technical elements, the training dives into what business users need to know to keep IT resources secure and protected. These scheduled sessions—which should last no more than 30 to 60 minutes—let people learn visually and practically and send a strong message about the importance of security.

Beyond employee training, information technology consultants can assist in conducting biannual, or at least annual, vulnerability assessments of a firm's technology infrastructure.

Mr. Scharfman: Compliance has increasingly become integrated with the information technology function. What perspective would you give to CCOs, who may not have extensive backgrounds in information technology, to help them develop technology-focused policies?

Mr. Paul: When developing technology-focused policies for a fund, it is important to appreciate and understand the following three items.

First, selecting the right service providers is one of the most critical decisions a fund will make. When it comes to outsourcing a business function—from technology to administration to accounting—it is imperative that firms do their due diligence and select a provider that can meet their unique requirements. To find and sustain success, firms should look to enter into trusted partnerships with key service providers—relationships that offer open lines of communication, flexibility, and, ultimately, trust and accountability.

Second, understand your firm's vulnerabilities and exposures. Cybersecurity is the single most talked about area of technology currently for businesses across the financial sector. At a minimum, a fund must understand the potential risks facing its operations and what safeguards are in place for protection. With both allocators and regulators asking detailed questions with regard to cybersecurity, funds must employ a comprehensive strategy to mitigate risk across the firm.

Finally, a firm must utilize an IT solution that can grow with it. This is a common mistake most funds make. Too often at launch, a fund manager assumes that they only require the bare minimum in terms of technology. This short-term thinking, rather than looking two years down the road, sets a firm up for challenges. Odds are, if a firm is consistently performing well, it is going to outgrow its current IT system and, therefore, require a much more complicated transition. By taking the time to think through what the firm needs down the line and implementing systems that can grow along with them, the firm is in much better shape to minimize the time and money spent on technology in the future.

Mr. Scharfman: How has the role of information technology consultants' services evolved over the last five years for hedge funds?

Mr. Paul: Today, information technology consultants play an increasingly important role in not only providing a technology infrastructure to a fund but also assisting in risk mitigation and policy development. From a security perspective, a firm's IT consultant may also be responsible for or involved in drafting information security policies and procedures to support security operations within the firm.

Data Backup, Archiving, and the Cloud

Mr. Scharfman: What are some of the best technology practices that a hedge fund compliance department can implement for backing up and archiving data?

Mr. Paul: Given that some regulatory requirements set time frames for record retention, having e-mail and instant message (IM) archiving in place helps complete technology infrastructure.

An archiving solution can assist funds in responding to any audits or litigation discovery requests in a timely manner. An ideal solution, for example, should be able to effectively handle electronic discovery requests by ensuring quick access to relevant data and avoiding disclosure of irrelevant, sensitive, or proprietary information. Following are some additional best practices for e-mail and instant message archiving that funds should consider:

- Retain e-mails and IMs for the prescribed amount of time by law
- Don't (only) use tape backups—in the event of a disruption or disaster, a fund should be prepared with another method of retention

- Store data in a Write Once Read Many (WORM) format that helps preserve message integrity and prevents alterations
- Allow for easy indexing and searching of files
- Keep archived data on your own server and make sure it can be accessed quickly if need be

Beyond archiving, regulatory and compliance organizations recognize the necessity of data security and advocate for firms to have a comprehensive backup solution in place. As such, data backup is an important element of a fund's overall data protection and security program especially as malicious ransomware attacks continue to increase.

In a ransomware attack scenario, hackers restrict access to infected computers by encrypting them and requiring that the victim pay a ransom in order to decrypt and recover their files. If a firm has recent backups, they can restore their data and avoid paying the ransom. It is worth noting that, in most cases, the disaster recovery environment will also be impacted by the malware because it maintains a mirror, real-time image of the production site.

Mr. Scharfman: Several years ago there were concerns among hedge funds with regard to the security of the cloud. Today, hedge funds have largely embraced usage of the cloud. Can you comment on how clouds have become more secure?

Mr. Paul: The hedge fund industry has embraced the use of cloud services, namely, private cloud platforms. One of the key advantages to cloud architectures also happens to be one of the most important considerations for financial services firms: risk mitigation—in particular, information security. That's quite important, given the increased focus the SEC has placed on cybersecurity safeguards, policies, and training.

An established private cloud provider can deploy the layers of cybersecurity protections that only the largest financial firms in the world can typically afford to implement, operate, and maintain. From the careful implementation of the principle of least privilege to comprehensive auditing and logging, and shutting off USB ports, to enforcing strong authentication methods, 24/7 perimeter monitoring for intrusions, vulnerability testing, and strong physical site-security, and more—the cloud vendor raises and fortifies the security posture of the fund to the levels that investors demand.

When it comes to disaster recovery, the cloud also presents significant advantages. That's because DR is an inherent design element of cloud computing. The cloud is predicated on multiple data centers, each deploying redundant servers and active-active network connections for transparent failover. This is managed by teams of highly trained professionals who should be testing that architecture regularly to virtually eliminate unplanned downtime. Geographic dispersion of the various data centers also means cloud vendors substantially reduce the risk of natural disasters or other catastrophic events with easy, transparent failover to active hot sites.

Mr. Scharfman: What types of cloud services are available to hedge funds today? How should they determine which type of cloud(s) to utilize?

Mr. Paul: Today, fund managers have a plethora of technology services and applications available to them via the cloud. From a complete managed IT platform and voice over IP (VoIP) to software as a service and managed service applications, the transition to cloud-based everything is well under way. Here are five key areas in which funds typically utilize the cloud.

First up is complete outsourcing of a firm's IT infrastructure, including file services, e-mail, mobility services, backup, and disaster recovery, to a private cloud provider. With this approach, the service provider is responsible for virtually everything, and IT costs are predictable. Typically, in today's market, start-up hedge funds are predominantly selecting a cloud platform at launch, while established funds are moving to the cloud during a technology refresh.

Another common cloud usage model is that of established firms utilizing the cloud for application hosting services. Firms are increasingly moving their applications, including Order Management (OMS), Risk, and CRM, to a hosted model. The benefits to adopting the hosted model include gaining a highly available infrastructure on which to run your applications, which is monitored and managed around the clock.

VoIP (or hosted voice cloud solutions) is a third way that firms are using the cloud. With business grade VoIP, funds eliminate the need for an on-site PBX and gain a cutting-edge, professionally managed voice solution while eradicating large up-front capital outlays and management challenges.

Managed cybersecurity, including Intrusion Detection and Prevention Monitoring, is an area gaining attention as funds become more aware of malicious threats. Using basic security tools is no longer an acceptable solution for growing hedge funds—particularly those seeking institutional money. By using a cloud service, firms can take advantage of a wide array of cloud security measures that are employed to protect their sensitive client data and resources. These cloud-based security practices range from physical security, isolation, and virtualization security to policy enforcement and access control, encryption, and resiliency.

Finally, firms are taking advantage of the disaster recovery services that a cloud solution provides. The ability to purchase cloud-based DR services has dramatically lowered the cost of entry for firms of all sizes. In the past, firms had to buy two of everything and then manage the duplicate environments. Cloud computing removes the responsibility of purchasing and managing a secondary site from the firm and delegates it to the cloud provider. Also, the complete data protection and business resiliency portfolios provided by the cloud enable hedge funds and alternative investment firms to utilize cloud computing to effortlessly protect themselves.

Information Protection and Cybersecurity

Mr. Scharfman: With regard to information protection and cybersecurity, hedge funds are increasingly developing Written Information Security Policies (WISP). What are some critical considerations for hedge funds in developing a WISP?

Mr. Paul: A WISP establishes a firm's plans and systems to protect personal information and company-sensitive data. A WISP typically includes both administrative and technical safeguards and identifies confidential information, where it is located, how it is protected, and who has access to it. Technical safeguards include an assessment of current policies, such as penetration software and encryption, and technical policies, such as password changes and access control.

Eze Castle Integration's team follows four stages when working with a client to create, maintain, and train employees on a WISP. First is the development stage. During this step of creating the WISP, the following items are covered:

- *Business Operations Assessment*: The process of identifying what systems and plans are currently being used to safeguard information and who can access the information
- *Technical Policy Assessment*: The evaluation of the technical procedures the firm goes through to protect data
- *Regulation Requirements*: In order to stay compliant with regulations and laws, firms must stay up-to-date on the legal environment and document legislation the firm must adhere to
- *Cybersecurity Incident Response Guidelines*: This part identifies who has responsibilities in the event of a breach, whether it is the Computer Security Incident Response Team and/or Chief Information Security Officer. A CSIRT team should be made up of both IT and business personnel so that both perspectives are addressed.
- *Third-Party Risk Assessment*: If your firm is using any third-party vendors, it is imperative that they understand what information they can access and security measures that they have in place to protect both your information and their own.
- *Employee Guidelines*: As employees can be any firm's weakest link, it is important to inform and educate internal staff on the policies and procedures included within a WISP and best practices for a smart security strategy.

We recommend funds conduct an audit on their WISP ideally annually. During the annual audit, the following items should be reviewed:

- *Assessment*: Every couple of years, take the time to review the existing policies and procedures in your WISP. Is everything still current? Have there been changes made to reflect changes in your business?
- *Reporting*: Report any exposures that should be addressed in the WISP and other recommendations made to ensure the protection of information.
- *Sample Documentation*: Create templates for third-party risk assessments and employee guidelines.

Employee training is critical to creating a culture of security awareness. Training components include:

- *Defining*: Employees and investors should have an understanding of what is deemed confidential information, for example, research notes, algorithms, the firm's financial status.
- *Computer Incident Response Team*: Creating a team on paper isn't enough; employees need to know and be trained in how they should react in the event that there is a breach.
- *Guidelines*: What are the procedures for company-owned equipment and how should an employee utilize those devices? Training in these areas could reduce the risk of a breach.
- *Internal versus External Threats*: Training employees on risks like social engineering, phishing, user error, and the loss of USB devices is critical because they need to know how to react in the event that something happens and how to employ certain practices to prevent them from happening in the first place.

A final state is maintenance. The financial industry landscape is ever-changing with new regulations, sophisticated hackers, and a turbulent market. To stay protected, firms must continuously update their WISP documentation, especially the summary, third-party assessments, and employee guidelines.

Mr. Scharfman: What are some of the common mistakes hedge fund compliance departments make in designing a WISP?

Mr. Paul: A common mistake funds make in designing a Written Information Security Policy is underestimating the importance of employee training and ongoing security awareness. With the proper training, education, and firm-wide support, employees can provide one of the most formidable and effective lines of defense against everything, from the savviest hackers to simple, everyday security exploits.

Annual employee security training is a must; however, it is also important to ensure employees receive a regular stream of information around data security. Keeping them updated with news about emerging threat strategies, for example, will reinforce the fund's security-oriented culture.

Mr. Scharfman: Financial regulators are increasingly focused on examining hedge fund cybersecurity preparedness. How should hedge fund compliance professionals think about cybersecurity? What steps should compliance departments take to meet their cybersecurity obligations?

Mr. Paul: Financial regulators have made it clear to fund managers through a variety of notices and risk alerts that significant security risks face the industry as a whole. As a result, those funds that have not yet created and implemented cybersecurity programs have potentially failed to address an area that has been a top regulatory issue. In fact, the SEC has noted security as one of the SEC's top exam priorities since 2014. While guidance from the SEC, the NFA, the CFTC and FINRA are not entirely in agreement, there is a common theme—funds must adopt a culture of cybersecurity compliance that permeates the entire organization. While these regulatory bodies have not defined the technology or program components that must be utilized, they have set the expectations that funds:

1. Do the initial work of assessing, designing and customizing such a program.
2. Follow through with continued efforts of integrating, testing, and monitoring that program for its effectiveness.

Mr. Scharfman: In regard to cybersecurity trends, can you provide some perspective on how cybersecurity threats to hedge funds have increased in recent years? What emerging cyber threats should hedge funds be most concerned about today?

Mr. Paul: Cybersecurity threats abound across the financial sector, and the sophistication of hackers is increasing. Some of the most common threats facing hedge funds present themselves in the form of phishing attacks and social engineering. Software vulnerabilities, often found in outdated software, are also key targets for hackers.

In a phishing scheme, for example, a hacker broadly disseminates a fraudulent e-mail with aim to acquire sensitive data, such as login credentials, IT resources, or banking information. The message may request the recipient submit personal information or click on a link embedded with malware. While this approach may not trick a sophisticated user, a distracted employee could make one mistake and compromise a firm's entire network.

A variation of this security threat is spear phishing. This technique uses a much more targeted approach and, increasingly, is used in the form of sophisticated bank wiring schemes. In a spear phishing incident, criminals target specific firms or individuals and conduct background research to compile employee names, titles, and contact information. Social networks are common resources crawled for this information. Obtaining such details and observing communications provides criminals with the tools to mirror e-mail addresses, website URLs, and dialect. The end result is the criminal's identity masqueraded as a legitimate, trustworthy source.

Increasingly, anyone can be a target and firms should train employees to recognize social engineering techniques. The differentiating factor between an authentic and fraudulent message could come down to one inversed letter. Prudence of employees in conjunction with a honed adeptness for security is one of the greatest defenses to help thwart attacks. Essentially the key to your firm's network, it is crucial that employees scrutinize any e-mail that inquires for information regarding login credentials and bank/wire transfers.

Mr. Scharfman: Some hedge funds actively engage with third-party vendors to conduct testing of the security of their networks through penetration testing, others either perform it in-house or not at all. Can you provide perspective on the benefits of third-party versus in-house penetration testing and the range of options available?

Mr. Paul: One question asked within an SEC cybersecurity questionnaire centers on whether a firm "conducts periodic risk assessments to identify cybersecurity threats, vulnerabilities, and potential business consequences," and if so, who conducts them and how often. A key driver behind this question is likely to ensure that firms take a proactive approach to security.

A common type of risk assessment associated with information technology and cybersecurity is an external vulnerability assessment. This essentially is the process of identifying and categorizing vulnerabilities related to a system or infrastructure. Typical steps included with a vulnerability scan or assessment include the following:

- Identifying all appropriate systems, networks, and infrastructures
- Scanning networks to assess susceptibility to external hacks and threats
- Classifying vulnerabilities based on severity
- Making tactical recommendations around how to eliminate or remediate threats at all levels

As a best practice, Eze Castle Integration recommends that funds conduct external vulnerability assessments at least once per year. Many firms may opt for semiannual scans, particularly if the firm's technology environment is continually changing.

The true goal of the vulnerability assessment is to gauge the level of security a firm has in place to protect against external threats and cyber-attacks.

Depending on the third party conducting the test, a firm may be graded with a number, or a letter score, or simply provided with a list of vulnerabilities and security recommendations.

Business Continuity and Disaster Recovery

Mr. Scharfman: In light of events such as Hurricane Sandy in the United States in 2012, financial regulators have focused on hedge fund's business continuity and disaster recovery (BCP/DR) plans. What assistance can information technology consultants, such as your firm, typically offer hedge funds in meeting their ongoing compliance requirements in this area?

Mr. Paul: When discussing effective business continuity and disaster recovery planning, it is important to understand the objective of the processes. First, these plans aim to provide an understanding of which procedures and personnel are essential. Second, they center on documenting, planning, implementing, testing, and maintaining the policies, procedures, and infrastructure to ensure that critical processes and essential personnel can continue to operate or quickly return to operations after an unexpected outage.

The role that information technology consultants, such as Eze Castle Integration, play ranges from crafting the business continuity plan and conducting employee training to delivering disaster recovery as a service or building a secondary disaster recovery site.

Creating a business continuity plan is a time-intensive process that can often take several months. The process includes interviewing the necessary parties and examining the collected information to establish a Risk Assessment and Business Impact Analysis for the fund. Then multiple drafts of the plan are developed and reviewed with key personnel to ensure all aspects of the business are accurately represented and protected. Once the plan is finalized, a firm should commit to testing and maintaining the finished plan at least annually. As with disaster recovery planning, only experience allows a business continuity planner to fully understand the interdependencies and nuances that ensure a plan will best protect a fund's essential operations and personnel.

Most hedge funds elect to hire a third party to assist with the development, implementation, and ongoing maintenance of the firm's business continuity plan. When it comes to formulating a DR strategy, one of the first items a fund must tackle is prioritizing their systems and conducting triage-style assessments about which data and applications are most important. These findings allow a firm to determine the recovery point and recovery time objectives for various applications, systems, and data sources. The recovery time objective (RTO) is the goal for the amount of time it would take to recover lost data or service. The RTO for mission-critical systems—such as trading—might be extremely short or nonexistent, while the RTO for a general ledger system might be several hours. Establishing recovery priorities will have implications on the DR design.

Finally, when talking about disaster recovery, it is important to understand that DR does not equal backup. As outlined earlier, DR replicates the production. If something occurs at the primary data center, you can resume operations in DR. However, if something is deleted in the production environment, that action is typically mirrored, thus deleted in DR as well. Backups, on the other hand, create an offline copy of your data that is not accessible except to restore, sometimes utilizing a third-party vendor to store that data in an alternate location. If access to a file was lost in both production and DR, backups grant the ability to recover the data.

Mr. Scharfman: What are some of the biggest mistakes you see hedge funds make in designing their BCP/DR plans?

Mr. Paul: Common mistakes we find around business continuity and DR plans center around:

- Not keeping applications up to date in the DR environment
- Not training employees on BCP/DR procedures
- Not testing the BCP/DR

Conducting DR tests at least twice per year can assist firms with addressing these common mistakes. Testing allows funds to validate that the applications in the DR site match the business needs. For example, is a recently added accounting system correctly configured in the DR site and ready for seamless failover should an outage occur? Beyond application validation, it is important to be realistic (during DR planning) about what applications require DR because adding a new application, such as an order management system, during a disaster isn't an option. Another benefit of testing is that it helps users get comfortable with the DR environment and login process.

Another mistake firms make is not having enough remote access (i.e., Citrix) licenses for all employees. Load testing is also an important aspect of the testing process as it helps guarantee your DR system can accommodate having all employees access it concurrently.

Mr. Scharfman: What measures can hedge funds take to mitigate their information security concerns surrounding having employees working remotely in the event of a BCP/DR event?

Mr. Paul: When it comes to remote access via the Internet in the event of a DR incident, the most commonly used methods for secure access are virtual private network (VPN) and Citrix. It is noteworthy that these connections should encrypt the data while in transit to protect it from third-party interception.

With a VPN connection, IPSec or SSL VPN technologies work by connecting a user's remote computer to their primary office desktop or hardware. The user is able to "remote desktop" and run all of the applications that live on the work computer's server or in the firm's cloud platform.

With a Citrix server, a user is able to log into a website via any computer and access the applications that live on the Citrix server in the firm's cloud platform or communication room. When a user clicks any application icon, it will appear as if it is running locally despite being housed on a remote server.

Additional secure remote access methods include enterprise-grade file sharing tools, such as Varonis DatAnywhere, which we provide to clients with our Eze Private Cloud service. It is important to note that employees should not use personal e-mail or public file sharing tools (i.e., Dropbox) for company business. These tools pose security risks and may violate company requirements around archiving, encryption, and protection of personal information.

CHAPTER SUMMARY

Interviews with representatives of a hedge fund compliance consulting firm and a hedge fund information technology consultant are featured. Trends in these areas of compliance are also discussed. These interviews highlight the integral role played by third-party service providers in developing and maintaining a hedge fund's compliance function. In the next chapter, we will continue our focus on the real-world compliance challenges facing hedge funds by outlining key trends and future developments.

CHAPTER 12

Trends and Future Developments

INTRODUCTION

Throughout this book, we have provided an overview of core hedge fund compliance concepts. We began with a general overview of key concepts and then focused on the role of regulators in enforcing compliance. Our discussion then proceeded to focus on the key players in compliance, including the Chief Compliance Officer (CCO) and the role of other compliance personnel. This analysis also covered the structure of a hedge fund's internal compliance organization as well as the role of other internal compliance mechanisms such as fund committees. Other key topics we addressed included the influence of technology on compliance, the role of service providers on compliance, and the investor evaluation of compliance functions. To demonstrate the practical application of these compliance principles in Chapter 9, we analyzed historical case studies in compliance. In this final chapter, we will look to emerging compliance trends that will shape the industry in the coming years.

In this chapter, we will discuss several leading compliance trends that have affected the compliance environment in recent years. Understanding and monitoring compliance and regulatory trends such as these will allow those involved with hedge funds to better anticipate the needs of the industry and to meet the ongoing challenges of this evolving, complex section of the hedge fund landscape.

CHIEF COMPLIANCE OFFICERS PERSONAL LIABILITY CONCERNS

An emerging trend involves the issue of personal liability surrounding the role of the CCO. Historically, in most cases if a hedge fund committed regulatory compliance violations, the fund management entity and not the CCO directly would be liable. More recently, questions have been raised regarding the extent to which CCOs should bear personal liability for their actions undertaken during the course of their work for a hedge fund.

Two SEC cases from 2015 that directly highlighted the issue of CCO liability in financial firms. Charges were brought in April 2015 against Black-Rock Advisors LLC. In that case, a BlackRock portfolio manager who oversaw energy-focused funds, Daniel J. Rice III, was working at BlackRock when at the same time he also founded Rice Energy, an oil and natural gas production company.[1] According to the SEC, Rice Energy formed a joint venture with a publicly traded coal firm named Alpha Natural Resources Inc. Eventually, Alpha was one of the largest holdings in the BlackRock fund managed by Mr. Rice. Although there is nothing inherently wrong with this arrangement, the SEC found that BlackRock's CCO at the time, Bartholomew Battista, caused the fund's failure to report a material compliance matter, namely, Mr. Rice's outside involvement with Rice Energy, to their boards of directors.[2] The SEC also found that BlackRock additionally failed to adopt and implement policies and procedures for outside activities of employees, and that Mr. Battista caused this failure.[3] Blackrock settled the charges and paid a $12 million penalty; Mr. Battista paid $60,000.[4]

The second case involved SFX Financial Advisory Management Enterprises, a subsidiary of concert promoter Live Nation, that specialized in providing financial management to professional athletes.[5] In this case, the SEC alleged that the firm's Chief Compliance Officer, Eugene S. Mason, failed to supervise the firm's former president, violated the custody rule, and made a false statement in an ADV filing, failed to conduct reviews of cash flows in client accounts as required by the firm's compliance policies, and did not perform an annual compliance review.[6] It was also alleged by the SEC that the firm's former president, Brian J. Ourand, stole approximately $670,000 over a five-year period by writing checks to himself and initiating wires from client accounts for his own benefit.[7] SFX settled the case for $150,000 and Mr. Mason paid $25,000.[8]

As can be expected, there are conflicting opinions on the issue of CCO personal liability. On the one hand, arguments have been raised by regulators that pursuing regulatory actions against CCOs directly actually benefits the hedge fund industry by eliminating bad actors and promoting the importance of the compliance role.[9] Others have argued that increased enforcement actions against hedge fund CCOs, coupled with sometimes vague compliance guidelines, creates an environment that disincentivizes well-meaning hedge fund compliance professional efforts for fear of increased liability.[10]

There is even dissent on this issue among regulators. In these two SEC cases, SEC commissioner Daniel M. Gallagher voted against the settlement actions involving the CCOs. His reasons included that he felt the settlements illustrated a concerning trend toward strict liability for CCOs and that the regulators themselves shared in the blame for potential CCO violations because the rules in place for CCOs were themselves not adequately clear.[11]

In addition, Mr. Gallagher highlighted the potential chilling effect that these types of regulatory actions, stating in part that they may send a *"troubling message that CCOs should not take ownership of their firm's compliance policies and procedures, lest they be held accountable for conduct that, under Rule 206(4)-7, is the responsibility of the adviser itself. Or worse, that CCOs should opt for less comprehensive policies and procedures with fewer specified compliance duties and responsibilities to avoid liability when the government plays Monday morning quarterback."*[12]

Mr. Gallagher also voiced concern for the effect that such actions could have on smaller investment advisers where there is often a commingling of compliance and business functions, and the CCO may unwittingly take ownership of business functions that could subject them to liability.[13]

It remains to be seen whether the objections raised by individuals such as Mr. Gallagher will have an effect on slowing the charge toward increasing liability for CCOs. Regardless of the threat of personal liability for CCOs, the enhanced attention by regulators paid to this issue should be reason enough for hedge funds, and their CCOs in particular, to focus even more intently on strict oversight of regulatory compliance obligations going forward.

INCREASED SENIOR MANAGER REGULATORY ACCOUNTABILITY

Related to the trend of CCO liability, another trend on the horizon for hedge fund senior management, including compliance professionals, relates to increased overall personal accountability to regulators. An example of this is the United Kingdom's Senior Manager Regime (SMR), which took effect on March 7, 2016. Under the SMR, senior managers at financial firms, as part of their application for approval with regulators, must now submit what is known as a statement of responsibility.[14] This document designates the areas that the senior managers are responsible for. If the regulators find out that there were compliance violations in those areas, action will be taken against the responsible individuals. It should also be noted that under the SMR there is a responsibility for the filings to be updated on an ongoing basis in the event an individual's responsibilities change.[15]

The implementation of the SMR is overseen by the Prudential Regulation Authority (PRA) and the Financial Conduct Authority (FCA), which at the same time also implemented an accompanying Conduct Rules and a Certification Regime (CR) to establish basic fit and proper professional standards for both senior managers and those in key risk functions that could pose "significant harm" to customers. Similar to one of the goals of Dodd-Frank in the United States, these UK regimes seek to increase personal accountability for compliance violations.

Although the regimes currently only apply to banks, building societies, credit unions, and PRA-designated investment firms, in 2018, the regimes covered will expand and at that time could encompass hedge funds as well.[16]

These types of initiatives, represent an increased global push by regulators to enhance the ownership of the compliance functions by hedge funds and will present an ongoing series of regulatory reporting and compliance risk assessment liability challenges going forward.

COMPLIANCE-RELATED INSURANCE

Another emerging trend relates to the increased use and cost of compliance-related insurance coverage for hedge funds. Hedge funds, like most businesses, maintain different types of insurance coverages and bonding. Some of this coverage may be required by the rules of the location(s) in which the hedge fund is based. A common example of this would be a requirement in states, such as New York, in which hedge funds employers purchase workers' compensation insurance.[17] Other types of coverage may depend on the types of assets the hedge fund manage. For example, a requirement under Section 412 of the U.S. Employee Retirement Income Security Act (ERISA) requires that a hedge fund maintain a fidelity bond when more than 25 percent of its assets come from special types of investors known as benefit plans.[18] Other types of insurance coverage may be optional, such as key person insurance and cybersecurity insurance. To deal with the increasing risk of cybersecurity threats, cyber insurance can provide coverage for certain damages associated with cyber data breaches and attacks.

Other popular types of insurance coverage commonly maintained by hedge funds is Errors & Omissions (E&O) and Director and Officer (D&O) coverages. The two types of policies are often grouped together under so-called professional liability insurance. Depending on the specifics of the policies issued to the hedge fund, professional liability E&O and D&O insurance can provide coverage for a wide variety of items. One of the more common areas in which hedge funds utilize these policies is to afford key fund personnel such as directors and officers as well as the investment adviser entity. E&O and D&O insurance typically provides coverage in the event of errors, omissions, and breaches of duty by covered individuals and entities. Another key feature is that the policies may provide a hedge fund, and select personnel, with coverage to cover the costs of mounting a legal defense against lawsuits in certain instances.

In recent years, regulatory agencies, such as the U.S. SEC and the UK FCA, as well as local U.S. state regulators, have increased their scrutiny of hedge funds. With this increased attention also comes increased litigation brought by these regulators as part of enforcement activity. To meet this growing demand, a recent trend has emerged whereby the hedge fund insurance industry has offered professional liability coverage to hedge fund managers that can provide them with coverage to cover the cost of mounting a legal defense when these regulatory actions are brought.

As with all insurance policies, there are a number of exceptions and specific requirements for a hedge fund to be eligible for the coverage. One of the key areas that influences whether a hedge fund will be eligible for coverage of their legal defenses when regulatory actions are brought relates to the issue of if a hedge fund ultimately admits guilt in a regulatory action. In recent years there has been increased pressure for hedge funds that enter into settlements with financial regulators such as the SEC to actually admit guilt, as opposed to entering into a settlement with the regulator in which they neither admitted nor denied guilt.[19] Insurance policies have been traditionally drafted so that legal costs are excluded if a hedge fund admits guilt. In the insurance industry these exclusions may be referred to as the final adjudication of a claim or judgment exceptions. While this specific issue is still developing, as regulators increase their enforcement efforts there is also a growing concern that hedge fund insurers will have to pay increased defense costs.[20] This, consequently, has many in the industry speculating that the costs of these policies to hedge funds will increase as well.

INCREASINGLY COORDINATED HEDGE FUND REGULATION IN EUROPE

The hedge fund industry has evolved to become global in nature, primarily through investments in multiple markets throughout the world. As global investing for hedge funds has matured—and hedge funds have sought to raise capital from investors all over the world—there is a need for increased sophistication in fund operations, accounting, managing the tax consequences of international investments, and the compliance implications of investing in multiple markets.

As part of these global efforts, hedge funds are increasingly subjected to the oversight of financial regulatory bodies in different locations around the world. To deal with these challenges, hedge funds have developed relationships with specialized service providers such as compliance consultants and law firms that can assist in navigating both country-specific regulatory rules, as well as work to assist a coordinated effort of global compliance.

In Europe, in particular, over the past few years a trend has emerged for regulators to better collaborate across the region rather than having each country's respective regulatory focus exclusively on oversight of a single country. Throughout Europe, this increased regulatory collaboration has brought both challenges and opportunities. As an example, the initiative known as the Alternative Investment Fund Managers Directive (AIFMD) passport structure brought with it increased marketing flexibility for certain European managers seeking to raise capital across most of Europe, while at the same time placing into question the ability of certain non-EU managers to market their funds in Europe.[21]

This regional collaboration by European regulators also has brought increased compliance requirements. A prime example of two newly emerging regulations in Europe that are going to present new compliance challenges are the Market Abuse Directive and Regulation (MAD/MAR) and the Markets in Financial Instruments Directive II (MiFID II or MiFID 2). Some of the new compliance requirements European hedge funds managers will need to comply with under MiFID II include more extensive recording of telephonic and e-mail communications, increased restrictions on research-related commission-sharing arrangements, and a host of increased reporting requirements. Somewhat concerning, a recent Bloomberg survey indicated that only 7 percent of those fund managers surveyed said their firms were ready to meet these record-keeping requirements, and nearly 50 percent said they would not be prepared to meet the January 3, 2017, deadline.[22] Recognizing the problem, the European Securities and Markets Authority (ESMA) opted to extend the MiFID 2 compliance deadline by one year, until January 3, 2018.[23]

While regional collaboration may ultimately allow for enhanced compliance efficiencies for hedge fund managers seeking to conduct business throughout Europe, it also brings with it significant compliance hurdles.

Going forward, both hedge fund managers based in Europe and those that seek to market their funds in Europe will likely need to increase the resources and time spent on ensuring that their compliance functions meet regulatory requirements not only on a country-specific basis but also throughout the region as well.

CHAPTER SUMMARY

The focus was on emerging hedge fund compliance trends. We began by discussing the trend of hedge fund regulators seeking to increasingly assign personal liability to CCOs for regulatory violations. Next, we highlighted a related trend of increased senior management accountability through the example of the UK's Senior Manager Regime. Another trend that was discussed is that hedge funds are increasingly focusing on insurance coverage related to compliance risks. This includes professional liability coverage to cover the costs of litigation defense related to regulatory actions. Finally, we outlined the trend of increasingly regionally focused hedge fund regulations in Europe through examples including the Alternative Investment Fund Managers Directive and the Markets in Financial Instruments Directive II.

NOTES

1. Jason Zweig and Kristen Grind, "BlackRock to Pay $12 Million Penalty for Failing to Disclose Conflict of Interest," press release, April 20, 2015.
2. U.S. Securities and Exchange Commission, "SEC Charges BlackRock Advisors with Failing to Disclose Conflict of Interest to Clients and Fund Boards," press release, April 20, 2015.
3. Ibid.
4. See Securities of Exchange Commission Administrative Proceeding File No. 3-16501, "In the Matter of BlackRock Advisors, LLC and Bartholomew A. Battista," www.sec.gov/litigation/admin/2015/ia-4065.pdf.
5. Mark Schoeff Jr., "Live Nation Subsidiary That Represented Mike Tyson Charged with Fraud by SEC," *Investment News*, June 16, 2015.
6. U.S. Securities and Exchange Commission, "Investment Advisory Firm's Former President Charged With Stealing Client Funds," press release, June 15, 2015.
7. Ben Conrack, "SEC Hits Fired Athlete Investment Exec for Theft From Clients," *Law360*, June 15, 2015.
8. See Securities and Exchange Commission Administrative Proceeding File No. 3-16591, "In the Matter of SFX Financial Advisory Management Enterprises, Inc. and Eugene S. Mason," www.sec.gov/litigation/admin/2015/ia-4116.pdf.
9. See A. Ceresney, "2015 National Society of Compliance Professionals, National Conference: Keynote Address," U.S. SEC, November 4, 2015.
10. Hazel Bradford, "Chief Compliance Officers Prepare for Closer SEC Scrutiny," *Pensions & Investments*, January 11, 2016.
11. C. Flood, "Compliance Officers Feel They Have a Target on Their Backs," *Financial Times*, June 21, 2015.
12. Commissioner Daniel M. Gallagher, "Statement on Recent SEC Settlements Charging Chief Compliance Officers with Violations of Investment Advisers Act Rule 206(4)-7," June 18, 2015, www.sec.gov/news/statement/sec-cco-settlements-iaa-rule-206-4-7.html.
13. Bradford, "Chief Compliance Officers Prepare for Closer SEC Scrutiny."
14. Financial Conduct Authority, "FCA Publishes Final Rules to Make Those in the Banking Sector More Accountable," press release, July 7, 2015.
15. COOConnect, "Working with the Bank of England's Senior Managers Regime," press release, May 31, 2016.

16. HM Treasury, "Senior Managers and Certification Regime: Extension to All FSMA Authorised Persons," press release, October 2015.
17. New York State Workers' Compensation Board, "Workers' Compensation Coverage," www.wcb.ny.gov/content/main/Employers/wclcompliance.jsp.
18. Virginia C. Smith, "Guidance Regarding ERISA Fidelity Bonding Requirements," memo, Field Assistance Bulletin No. 2008-04, U.S. Department of Labor, November 25, 2008.
19. See Alexandra Stevenson, "Falcone to Admit to Wrongdoing as S.E.C. Takes a Harder Line," *DealBook*, August 19, 2013.
20. Judy Greenwald, "SEC Policy Could Lead to Higher Defense Costs, D&O Insurance Rate Hikes," *Business Insurance*, October 6, 2013.
21. COOConnect, "Uncertainty over Extent to Which AIFMD Passport Will Be Afforded to Non-EU Managers," press release, February 16, 2015.
22. Harald Collet, "Gearing up for MiFID II," *Bloomberg Vault* (blog), January 5, 2016.
23. European Commission, "Commission Extends by One Year the Application Date for the MiFID II Package," press release, February 10, 2016.

About the Author

Jason Scharfman is the Managing Partner of Corgentum Consulting, a specialist consulting firm that performs operational due diligence reviews and background investigations of fund managers of all types, including hedge funds, private equity, real estate, and long-only funds on behalf of institutional investors, including pensions, endowments, foundations, fund of funds, family offices, and high-net-worth individuals.

He is recognized as one of the leading experts in the field of due diligence and is the author of *Hedge Fund Governance: Evaluating Oversight, Independence, and Conflicts* (Academic Press, 2014), *Private Equity Operational Due Diligence: Tools to Evaluate Liquidity, Valuation, and Documentation* (John Wiley & Sons, 2012), and *Hedge Fund Operational Due Diligence: Understanding the Risks* (John Wiley & Sons, 2008). He has also contributed to the Chartered Alternative Investment Analyst (CAIA) curriculum on due diligence and has served on the organization's Due Diligence, Risk Management, and Regulation Committee.

Before founding Corgentum, Mr. Scharfman previously oversaw the operational due diligence function for a $6 billion alternative investment allocation group called Graystone Research at Morgan Stanley. While at Morgan Stanley, he was also a senior member of a team that oversaw all of Morgan Stanley's hedge fund operational due diligence efforts, allocating in excess of $13 billion to a firm-wide platform of more than 300 hedge fund managers across multiple investment strategies. Before joining Morgan Stanley, he held positions that primarily focused on due diligence and risk management within the alternative investment sector at Lazard Asset Management, SPARX Investments and Research, and Thomson Financial.

Mr. Scharfman received a BS in finance with an additional major in Japanese from Carnegie Mellon University, an MBA in finance from Baruch College's Zicklin School of Business, and a JD from St. John's University School of Law. He is admitted to the practice of law in New York and in New Jersey. In addition, he holds the Certified Fraud Examiner (CFE) and Certified in Risk and Information Systems Control (CRISC) credentials. He has consulted with the U.S. House Judiciary Committee on hedge fund regulation. He has also provided training to financial regulators on hedge fund due diligence. Mr. Scharfman has served as a consultant and testified as an expert in hedge fund litigation and has lectured on the subject of hedge fund operations and operational risk as an adjunct professor at New York University. He is a member of several industry organizations, including the Information Systems Audit and Control Association, the American Bar Association, the New York State Bar Association, and the New Jersey State Bar Association. He has written extensively on the subject of operational due diligence and speaks worldwide on due diligence and operational risks.

Index

Printed and bound by CPI Group (UK) Ltd, Croydon, CR0 4YY

16/04/2025

14658455-0001